Founder of the international women's rights organization Equality Now, **Jessica Neuwirth** is the former director of the New York Office of the United Nations High Commissioner for Human Rights. She is the founder and director of the recently formed ERA Coalition and of Donor Direct Action, an initiative to support women's rights organizations around the world. A graduate of Yale College and Harvard Law School, she lives in New York City.

**Gloria Steinem** is a world-renowned feminist organizer and writer who co-founded a variety of organizations in the American women's liberation movement, including *Ms.* magazine, the Ms. Foundation for Women, and the National Women's Political Caucus. Her books are published in the United States and other countries. In recent years, she helped found the Women's Media Center, Donor Direct Action, and the ERA Coalition. She travels widely in the United States and around the world as a speaker and organizer. In 2013, she was awarded the Presidential Medal of Freedom. She lives in New York City.

One of many buttons from the 1970s ERA campaign highlighting its patriotism.

# EQUAL MEANS EQUAL

## Why the Time for an
## Equal Rights Amendment Is Now

Jessica Neuwirth

With a foreword by Gloria Steinem

**THE NEW PRESS**

NEW YORK
LONDON

Requests for permission to reproduce selections from this book should be mailed to:
Permissions Department, The New Press, 120 Wall Street, 31st floor, New York, NY
10005.

Published in the United States by The New Press, New York, 2015

Distributed by Perseus Distribution

LIBRARY OF CONGRESS CATALOGING-IN-PUBLICATION DATA

Neuwirth, Jessica, author.
    Equal means equal : why the time for an equal rights amendment is now /
Jessica Neuwirth ; foreword by Gloria Steinem.
        pages   cm
    Includes bibliographical references.
    ISBN 978-1-62097-039-3 (paperback) — ISBN 978-1-62097-048-5 (e-book)
    1.  Equal rights amendments—United States.   I.  Title.
    KF4758.N48   2015
    342.7308'78—dc23                    2014029578

The New Press publishes books that promote and enrich public discussion and
understanding of the issues vital to our democracy and to a more equitable world. These
books are made possible by the enthusiasm of our readers; the support of a committed
group of donors, large and small; the collaboration of our many partners in the
independent media and the not-for-profit sector; booksellers, who often hand-sell
New Press books; librarians; and above all by our authors.

www.thenewpress.com

*Book design and composition by dix!*
*This book was set in Scala*

Printed in the United States of America

10   9   8   7   6   5   4   3   2   1

This book is dedicated to my mother, Gloria Neuwirth, who graduated from Yale Law School in 1958 only to be told when she interviewed with a New York law firm, "We don't hire women, but you're a pretty girl so we'd be happy to talk to you." The bar association would not hire her—they said they couldn't hire a woman because they had evening meetings. Today, at the age of eighty, she is working full time as a partner in the law firm of Davidson, Dawson & Clark. She is named in Best Lawyers in America and has been listed among New York Super Lawyers for the past seven years running. She is the best mother anyone could ever hope for, and I am eternally grateful for her unconditional support in every way. I also want to pay tribute to my late father, Robert S. Neuwirth, who gave me every opportunity in the world.

# CONTENTS

# ACKNOWLEDGMENTS

I want to pay tribute to the many courageous women who have suffered the injustice of discrimination and taken action to defend and promote the fundamental right to sex equality. I hope to honor the memory of Rebecca, Katheryn, and Leslie Gonzales, three beautiful girls from Colorado who lost their lives at the ages of ten, eight, and seven because our law failed to protect them from the deadly violence of their father, and failed again to deliver justice to their mother, Jessica Gonzales (now Lenahan), following this tragedy.

Special thanks to Catharine MacKinnon, Robin Morgan, and Gloria Steinem, whose brilliance has been a constant source of inspiration to me and countless others. They have guided me over the past twenty years in all my endeavors and have helped me tremendously with this book, for which I am deeply grateful. It is truly an honor to work with them and be part of a vision they have done so much to forge, and continue to advance, for the benefit of women across the country and around the world.

This book is based on extensive research done over the past year by Paul, Weiss, Rifkind, Wharton and Garrison, with great thanks to the firm and to Maria Vullo, Liza Velazquez, Erin Smith Dennis, and the rest of the team who have served as pro bono counsel to the Coalition for the ERA.

Thanks also to Chai Feldblum, Roberta Francis, Kamala Lopez, and Eleanor Smeal for taking the time to read drafts of this book and share their comments and advice with me, and to Dina Bakst, Taina Bien-Aimé, Jane Connors, Elizabeth Evatt, Bettina Hager, Kyung-wha Kang, Jane Levikow, Leanne Littrell DiLorenzo, Laura Neuwirth, Navi Pillay, Diane Rosenfeld, Richard Rothman and Melissa Salten, Pamela Shifman, Linda Wharton, and Liz Young. Thanks to Lauren Turner and Elizabeth Hague for research assistance.

It is a privilege to have this book published by The New Press, a unique publishing company I have long admired. I want to particularly thank Diane Wachtell, as well as Jed Bickman, Julie Enszer, and Sarah Fan for guiding me through the process of writing a book for the first time.

# FOREWORD

## Gloria Steinem

*People could make it against flood and pestilence, but not against the laws;*
*they went under.*

—Jorge Amado

Once upon a time, I believed that as an American, I was protected by the Constitution. When my schoolbooks cited it as the founding document of democracy, I assumed that everyone was equal before the law. Of course, I knew that the Constitution hadn't ended slavery or included women—not even the wives, daughters, and mothers of the Founding Fathers. Still, I assumed those wise men were doing the best they could in their time. After all, even ancient Athens—the birthplace of democracy, according to my schoolbooks—had slavery and no role for women other than housewife, courtesan, or slave.

It took centuries of revolt to open up our incomplete democracy. Slavery was ended by a Civil War; the Constitution was amended so once-enslaved men could vote; and another half-century was spent marching, lobbying, and going on hunger strikes before white and black women could vote. Even then, Southern states kept black women and men away from the polls with violence, and it took a long and brave civil rights movement to get the federal government to enforce its own laws. Today, a patchwork of state laws still makes it more confusing and difficult to vote in this country than in any other developed democracy in the world. Voter turnout is lower here than in, say, India, with all its poverty and illiteracy. Recently, officials from Ohio to Texas and North Carolina have manipulated rules to keep the less powerful out of the voting booth, the one place on earth where they could equal the powerful. As I write this, the League of Women Voters has just successfully challenged the Republican-dominated Florida state legislature for redrawing congressional districts to benefit Republicans.

Still, I got a human view of the Founding Fathers only from African American history, women's history, Native American history—everything I think of as remedial history—courses that still have to be sought out. The insights from these full-circle perspectives rarely get into the popular media.

For instance, many people don't know that slavery was condemned long before the Civil War. Owning slaves was a hot topic of debate at the Constitutional Convention itself. Some Founding Fathers called it an abomination, and others threatened to walk out unless it was accepted as an economic necessity and an institution found in the Bible. As for the total exclusion of white and free black women, any debate about that seemed confined to the domestic sphere, as were women themselves. Abigail Adams is usually quoted as only writing mildly to her husband, John Adams, "Remember the Ladies." Actually, she wrote him a threatening letter: "Do not put such unlimited power into the hands of the husbands. Remember, all men would be tyrants if they could . . . we are determined to foment a Rebellion, and will not hold ourselves bound by any laws in which we have no voice or representation." [1]

Rebellious women had allies among influential advisers, but since no women were allowed into the Constitutional Convention, they may not have known it. Now even the advisers have been neglected in history. Benjamin Franklin, who had been an ambassador to several Native nations and so understood more about them than the other Founders, invited two advisers from the Iroquois Confederacy to come to Philadelphia. Known to its members as the Haudenosaunee, or the People of the Longhouse, the Iroquois Confederacy was founded at least four centuries before Columbus arrived and included six of the major Native nations in North America. Power derived from "We, the People," who met in layers of talking circles. There was no concept of slavery, women were fully included, each member nation had autonomy over its own affairs, and decisions affecting the confederacy were made mutually. Since the thirteen colonies were also striving for a central government with local autonomy, leaders of the confederacy suggested the colonies adopt a similar confederate structure. That the Iroquois Confederacy became a model for the U.S. Constitution was finally acknowledged by a U.S. Senate Resolution in 1988. The Iroquois Confederacy is now believed to be the longest-lasting and oldest participatory democracy in the world, one far more inclusive and also less dependent on military force than Athens was.

When the two Native advisers arrived in Philadelphia, they gave John Hancock, president of the Continental Congress, an Indian name as a gesture of friendship. They also asked one question: *Where are your women?*

I wonder if Thomas Jefferson was responding to them when he famously said, "Were our State a pure democracy, there would still be excluded from our deliberations women who, to prevent deprivation or morals and ambiguity of issues, should not mix promiscuously in gatherings of men."[2]

I also read *An American Dilemma*, the landmark study of slavery and its legacy by the Nobel Prize–winning Swedish economist and sociologist Gunnar Myrdal. In an obscure appendix, he explained that enslaved people brought here from Africa were given the legal status of wives as the "nearest and most natural analogy."[3] All were chattel. Female children were the property of fathers or male guardians, and after marriage females died a "civil death" because husband and wife were one person, and that person was the man. Lawyers of the day argued that a wife could no more sue her husband than a man could sue himself. There were life-and-death differences, but neither enslaved people nor any women had a legal right to their own children, to any earnings from their work, to go to school, to enter an agreement, to appear in public, or to leave their masters' homes without danger of being legally and forcibly returned. Though abolitionists supported the Underground Railroad of enslaved people escaping the South, some condemned Susan B. Anthony for helping wives and children escape brutal husbands and fathers. As Paul the Apostle said in the Bible, "Wives, submit yourselves unto your husbands as unto the Lord." This and other religious justification of female subservience so outraged Elizabeth Cady Stanton that she gathered a team of twenty-six women, rewrote the Scriptures, and published the Woman's Bible—a book so controversial that it damaged her reputation and almost sank the suffrage movement.

Even up to the 1940s—a century after the end of slavery and a half-century after women won the vote—Myrdal could report, "In drawing a parallel between the position of, and feeling toward, women and Negroes we are uncovering a fundamental basis of our culture."[4]

So what did I learn from this more human view of the Constitution and its framers? I began to realize that the greatest gift of the Founding Fathers was not democracy, but the contagious *idea* of democracy, not a perfect Constitution, but one that could keep changing. Indeed, they may have recognized their own imperfections better than we do. For instance, the Founders not only rejected Europe's model of lifetime leadership but also elected leaders for limited terms and made them impeachable during those terms, as in the Iroquois Confederacy. The Constitution itself could be amended. Its first ten amendments, known as the Bill of Rights—freedom of speech, assembly, religion, and other protections for the individual—were added just after the Framers had finished the Constitution, and then realized it dealt with the state but not citizen power against the state. They went back and fixed it.

I wondered: what would have happened if the Founders actually had looked like the country? I think the Bill of Rights would have included reproductive freedom. After all, black women were forced to bear children who became slave labor, and white women were so pressured to populate a white country that on the frontier the average family was a two-mother family: the first wife died from too many childbirths, and the second wife cared for those children and gave birth to more. Early tombstones show the reason why women's life expectancy was far shorter than men's: *died at seventeen in childbirth . . . died at twenty leaving six beloved children. . . .*

This was so common that shocked Native American women referred to European American women as *those who die in childbirth*. Native societies were based on a balance between women and men, people and nature, and a traditional knowledge of herbs, abortifacients, and timing allowed women to decide when and whether to give birth. In the Europe that colonial women had come from, 6 to 8 million women healers had been murdered as witches over a period of three to five centuries, thus wiping out their knowledge and allowing patriarchal religions to control reproduction. In upstate New York, for instance, European women knew their Native neighbors and even had Sunday dinners with Seneca women, thus discovering Native birthing methods and cultures that may have inspired the suffrage movement. I bet Native women would have included reproductive freedom in the Bill of Rights and women as full citizens in the Constitution.

After women finally won the right to vote in 1920, the next step was prohibiting discrimination based on sex in almost every arena, from serving on juries to entering into financial transactions, and that required an Equal Rights Amendment. Though the Fourteenth Amendment promised "equal protection under the law," it had been passed in the wake of the Civil War with no intent or instance of including sex. In the late 1920s a group of suffragettes led by Alice Paul drafted the text for a constitutional amendment that would make sex a suspect category, along with race, religion, and national origin. But the movement never got off the ground and never came to a formal vote in Congress. The fight for an ERA would never be easy. For instance, unions had opposed the ERA because they saw it as in conflict with protectionist measures they had won for women workers. Even First Lady Eleanor Roosevelt sided with the unions, not equality. It wasn't until the Second Wave of feminism in which feminism was reborn in the 1960s that these protections were either eliminated as unnecessary or expanded to apply to men, too. Then the twenty-six simple words of the ERA became a battle cry again: *Equality of rights under the law shall not be abridged by the United States or by any state on account of sex.*

I and countless others entered into this struggle: testifying in Congress, cheering in 1972 when the ERA finally earned the two-thirds majority in Congress necessary for a constitutional amendment, and campaigning state by state for ratification by the required minimum of thirty-eight state legislatures. Congress had imposed a seven-year deadline on ratifying the ERA, and only after much additional campaigning would the deadline be extended to ten years. Meanwhile, thirty states ratified within the first two years, and that lulled the pro-ERA forces into a false sense of security. This was often compounded by our own error in seeing the ERA as an old and uncontroversial thing instead of what it was and is: a major way of redistributing wealth by requiring fairness for the biggest unpaid and underpaid workforce in the country—women of all races.

But right-wing economic and religious forces woke up to this danger. They began a national anti-ERA campaign with two major, if contradictory, arguments. First, they argued that the ERA would damage, not help women: it would integrate bathrooms; send women into the draft and combat; eliminate support for homemakers; require birth control and abortion by encouraging women to enter the paid labor force; legalize gay marriage; and generally destroy the family, society, and, in the right-wing view, Western civilization as we know it. Second, the ERA was not needed because women were already equal under the Constitution.

Neither argument was true. Both were effective. A major reason was that not one major newspaper, radio network, news service, or national television network did an independent investigative report on what the ERA actually would and would not do. Media were content to give equal time to each side and create debates with far more heat than light. Often the viewer or reader was more confused after watching the coverage than before. Indeed, surveys showed that journalistic coverage of the ERA actually *increased* confusion. Reporting rarely included the Amendment's twenty-six words, though in public opinion polls, over 60 percent of Americans supported them when they read them. In the end, the Equal Rights Amendment fell just three states short of the thirty-eight required to get it into the Constitution. It was pronounced dead—at least in that process—in 1982.

In retrospect, I think the anti-ERA forces succeeded for a mix of reasons. First, they knew very well that equality would cost a lot of money, from equal pay itself to equalizing actuarial tables and insurance rates, and they were motivated to stop it. Second, they had crucial influence in many state legislatures where business interests reign. For instance, insurance was the last major national industry regulated by state, not federal, government, so the insurance lobby often had great power there. Indeed, the most frequent occupation of a state legislator was insurance agent, whose company profits would be diminished by eliminating sex-based actuarial tables. Third, many or most anti-ERA women were operating out of an unfounded but well-cultivated fear that the ERA would weaken rather than strengthen their ability to be supported as dependent homemakers or to get child support if divorced. They gave the press an image of women against women.

We in the pro-ERA majority also share blame. First, most Americans didn't (and still don't) know the names of their own state legislators, much less how they vote. Most Americans were (and still are) even less likely to vote in state elections than in national ones. This leaves the majority vulnerable to a focused minority. There is also little understanding that state legislatures draw and redraw congressional districts, thus influencing the House on everything. (The Senate tends to represent majority views better because you can't redistrict a state.) Second, we were so focused on each state that we may not have run enough of a national campaign, and people see more national than local media. In public, Phyllis Schlafly, previously a little-known veteran of the John Birch Society and several unsuccessful political campaigns, was the face of the anti-ERA campaign. Because she was pretty much the only female foe of the ERA the media knew, you might say she was an artificial creation of the Fairness Doctrine, whose requirement that broadcasters air opposing views in controversial issues (regardless of their validity). It was appearing opposite a variety of ERA supporters that led to Schlafly's fame. (In my experience, a media interviewer would call and say, "Bring an anti with you.") Indeed, as I write this in 2014, Schlafly is still being interviewed about the issue and told one reporter that the pay gap between women and men should *increase*—not only because women don't choose the "difficult" jobs but also because women prefer to marry men who earn more than they do.

Third, and perhaps most important, most Americans, women and men, just didn't (and still don't) know the practical improvements the ERA would make in our daily lives. This is the great value of the book before you. *Equal Means Equal* explains in a clear and compelling way why the Equal Rights Amendment continues to be needed. It tells you in practical terms how it could be used to create more equality and justice in the daily lives of millions of Americans, both women and men.

Once you read it, I think you, too, will see the ERA as crucial to Americans of all races and economic groups. It's about time.

To brace you for the biases implicit in some of the arguments against the ERA, here are two examples from my past experience. First, from *The Thunderbolt*, a publication of the National States Rights Party: "Laws requiring men and women to be separated in prison would be invalidated [by the ERA]. A Negro judge has already used these equality laws in Chattanooga to lock a White woman in the same cell with a black man. She was then raped." Obviously, the right to privacy would prevail and the ERA would not integrate prisons or bathrooms—and doesn't in states with statewide ERAs—but this argument should prepare you for the intertwining of sexist and racist fears of equality. Second, from a Florida anti-ERA television commercial: scenes from a Miami Dolphins football game represented America without the ERA, and then footage of the San Francisco Gay Pride Parade represented America with the ERA. As outrageous as the TV ad itself was the fact that anti-ERA forces didn't have to pay a sympathetic TV station that ran it free on the false grounds that equal *unpaid* time was required to balance *paid* time that local ERA groups had spent months fundraising for.

It's also true that the grassroots support for the ERA created a decade of marches and rallies in Washington that rivaled the first one I ever witnessed: the famous march led by Martin Luther King Jr. in 1964. Now, in the age of the Internet as an organizing tool plus a better understanding of how deep inequality cuts, there are opportunities for such massive marches in every state capital.

Most of all, this book will break through the artificial smokescreen of false confidence that the Founding Fathers were omniscient, this is the most perfect democracy, any inequality is due to personal fault, and the Constitution protects us against all injustice.

The truth is that our democracy is a work in progress. We are all its Founders. We are all learning that we are linked and not ranked.

Since we also know that long before the Founding Fathers a greater equality existed on this same land, we can create it again.

# EQUAL MEANS EQUAL

# INTRODUCTION

Christy Brzonkala, Doris Garcia, Jessica Gonzales, and Tracy Rexroat are a few of the many American women who have suffered greatly over the past twenty years from sex discrimination in its various forms. They have all turned to the law in search of justice, and they have all been denied justice—for pay discrimination, pregnancy discrimination, and gender-based violence.

Unlike most other countries in the world, the United States does not have a constitutional equality provision guaranteeing equal rights for women. Supreme Court Justice Antonin Scalia has cynically affirmed, "Certainly the Constitution does not require discrimination on the basis of sex. The only issue is whether it prohibits it. It doesn't." [1] Supreme Court Justice Ruth Bader Ginsburg has expressed her wish to see this prohibition added to the Constitution and has publicly stated the hope that in her lifetime she will see women "get fired up about the Equal Rights Amendment." [2] The goal of this book is to help women and men get fired up enough about the absence of this fundamental human right to put it into the Constitution once and for all.

Alice Paul drafted the first Equal Rights Amendment (ERA) in the early twentieth century. She was one of the founders of the National Woman's Party, which had worked for passage of the Nineteenth Amendment granting women the right to vote. Alice Paul was a Republican, but the National Woman's Party was nonpartisan. Raised a Quaker, Alice Paul attributed her commitment to her faith. "When the Quakers were founded," she explained, "one of their principles was and is equality of the sexes. So I never had any other idea . . . the principle was always there." [3] Alice Paul was among those who picketed outside the White House for women's suffrage, starting in 1917. After months of what was one of the country's first organized nonviolent civil actions for social change, she and other women demonstrators were arrested and imprisoned for "obstructing traffic." They went on hunger strikes and endured forced feeding and beatings by prison

Alice Paul, a founder of the National Woman's Party, who first drafted the
Equal Rights Amendment in 1923. (Courtesy of Records of the National Woman's
Party, Manuscript Division, Library of Congress, Washington, D.C.)

guards. The brutality of this treatment increased public support for the cause of women's suffrage, and in 1920 the Nineteenth Amendment was adopted.

Alice Paul then turned her attention to the Equal Rights Amendment, which was introduced in Congress in 1923 to ensure that not only suffrage but all rights would be guaranteed equally to women and men. Representative Daniel Anthony of Kansas, a nephew of suffragist leader Susan B. Anthony, introduced the bill.[4] For more than twenty years after its introduction, the ERA was the subject of political debate and legislative deliberations, but it failed to galvanize support and never came to a vote in Congress. Early opposition came from some progressives, who feared it would do away with hard-won protective labor laws for women.

Over time, support grew slowly and the ERA was included in the political platforms of the Republican Party in 1940 and the Democratic Party in 1944. In 1946 the ERA came to the Senate floor for the first time, where it won a majority of votes but not the two-thirds required to pass a constitutional amendment. Beginning in the 1950s, support for both the proposed amendment and the principle of women's equality grew steadily, reinforced by the passage of the Equal Pay Act in 1963 and the Civil Rights Act in 1964, as well as the growing political power of the women's movement. Presidents Eisenhower, Kennedy, Johnson, Nixon, Ford, and Carter all endorsed the ERA.

In 1970, Representative Martha Griffiths organized sufficient bipartisan support to get the ERA out of the House Judiciary Committee, despite the opposition of committee chair Emanuel Celler, using a rare procedural move known as a "discharge petition." The House passed the bill by a two-thirds majority, but the Senate bill did not make it to the floor by the end of the session. In the next session of Congress, the ERA was passed decisively by both the House (354–24) and the Senate (84–8) on March 22, 1972, with a seven-year deadline for ratification by the states. Article V of the Constitution requires ratification of an amendment by three-fourths of the states (thirty-eight out of fifty).

The text of the ERA, which Alice Paul had rewritten in 1943 to replace her original wording, was a straightforward guarantee of legal equality for women and men:

*Section 1*: Equality of rights under the law shall not be denied or abridged by the United States or by any state on account of sex.

*Section 2*: The Congress shall have the power to enforce, by appropriate legislation, the provisions of this article.

*Section 3*: This amendment shall take effect two years after the date of ratification.

Initially states rushed to support the ERA. Less than one hour after its passage in Congress, Hawaii ratified the amendment. Within the first year, twenty-two states had ratified the ERA.[5] Eight more states ratified it in 1973.[6] However, a backlash then started to set in. In 1974, only three states ratified the ERA, and in 1975 only one state did so.[7] Over the next four years only one additional state ratified the ERA, in 1977, bringing the total to thirty-five.[8] Meanwhile, five states voted to rescind their ratification, starting in 1973, with more following suit in 1974.[9] When it became clear by 1978 that the thirty-eight states needed for ratification would be very difficult to reach by the expiration of the seven-year time limit in 1979, legislation was passed by Congress to extend the deadline to June 30, 1982.

In 1980, the Republican Party dropped the ERA from its platform, and Ronald Reagan came out against it, although his daughter Maureen Reagan, also a Republican, continued to campaign intensively across the country for the ERA. During the three additional years before the extended deadline, not a single additional state voted to ratify the ERA despite mass mobilization by the women's movement. Unions, religious groups, civic organizations, and trade associations all came together for the campaign—teachers, nurses, librarians, nuns, steelworkers, businesswomen, journalists, and more.

Like the suffragists who came before them, ERA supporters marched, picketed, fasted, and chained themselves to the gates of various halls of power. Presidents Ford and Carter issued a joint call for ratification. First Lady Rosalynn Carter actively supported ratification, and former First Ladies Betty Ford and Lady Bird Johnson participated in rallies organized by the National Organization for Women (NOW).[10]

Supporters of the Equal Rights Amendment march down Pennsylvania Avenue, August 26, 1977. (AP Photo)

Betty Ford served as co-chair of the ERA Countdown Campaign, together with the actor Alan Alda. There were close votes in North Carolina, Florida, and Illinois during this final push, but at the expiration of the extended ratification deadline in 1982, the ERA remained three states short of the thirty-eight needed to put it into the Constitution.[11]

Why was the decade-long effort from 1972 to 1982 to get the ERA ratified unsuccessful? In retrospect, what is striking is how very close to success it came. Several nationwide polls in 1981 and 1982 confirmed that a solid majority of Americans supported the ERA. State polls at the time, even in states that had not ratified the ERA, such as North Carolina, Florida, and Illinois, also showed consistent and solid majority support for the amendment.[12] As Eleanor Smeal, president of NOW at the time, recalled, "We were just a handful of votes away from victory in three states."[13]

For many people, the right-wing political activist Phyllis Schlafly was the face of opposition to the Equal Rights Amendment. She orchestrated anti-ERA activism through her organization, the Eagle Forum, and its STOP ERA offshoot, using fear tactics in an effort to mobilize women and men against the amendment. What were the fears at the time? Fear of women in combat, fear of unisex bathrooms, fear of gay rights, and the unimaginable prospect of same-sex marriage all fed the flames.

Although she herself was a lawyer, Phyllis Schlafly proclaimed that a woman's place was in the home by her husband's side, and she warned homemakers that they would lose the emotional and financial security of marriage. She announced proudly at meetings that she had permission from her husband to be present and whipped up venomous opposition to the ERA. In Illinois, where a three-week hunger strike just before the ratification deadline led to the hospitalization of some ERA supporters, anti-ERA women ate chocolate in front of the fasters and held signs with messages such as: "Evil, Rebellious, Agitators, the Communists, lesbians, and homosexuals, and those who work to destroy America and the right to be a true wife and homebuilder are for the ERA."[14]

It's hard to imagine today, more than thirty years later, that these fear tactics could be used with any effect and that they made putting equal rights for women into the Constitution so controversial in some states. Much has changed. Now, the growing number of women in the armed forces *want* the right to engage in combat and fear that their exclusion from combat, just recently overturned by the Department of Defense, is keeping them from reaching the highest levels of military rank. They want to be recognized for their service and sacrifice. Unisex bathrooms are everywhere and no longer can be used to inspire fear. Marriage equality for gay couples is increasingly recognized as a fundamental right, with support from the Supreme Court and legislation/litigation in a growing number of states. Last but not least, economic security in marriage has turned out to be way less secure than women thought when they campaigned against the ERA to preserve this illusion. Women are increasingly facing many obstacles to economic independence and security, which would more likely be helped rather than hindered by the ERA.

When talking to women and men about the ERA these days, one doesn't find much argument against it. The resistance, if it exists, is more passive, and it is somewhat mystifying that Phyllis Schlafly drew support from any women for her vision of women as dependent and

Activists Gloria Steinem and Dorothy Pitman Hughes, co-founders of the Women's Action Alliance in 1971, who toured the country together to promote women's rights. (Dan Wynn/Courtesy of Demont Photo Management)

subservient. The women's movement forged around the campaign for the ERA went on in the next thirty years to change the face of America and give women more power than they have ever had before. The 1980 slogan "We will remember in November!" sparked a growing recognition of the gender gap at the polls, and there has been a strong and steady increase in the numbers of women elected to political office, corporate boards, and other historically male-only institutions. In 1982 there were 23 women in Congress—by 2014, the number had more than quadrupled to 102.[15]

In light of this progress, the question often asked is "Do we really need the ERA? What would it change?" Many Americans—72 percent, according to a 2001 poll—think equal rights for women and men are already guaranteed by the Constitution.[16] This misconception is often followed by a renewed sense of outrage at the news that they aren't.

Many people seem to remember vaguely that the ERA "passed" without remembering that, for lack of ratification by just three more states, it failed to enter into force as a constitutional amendment. Very few people today argue against the ERA as a matter of principle. According to a poll in 2012, 91 percent of Americans think the Constitution should include equal rights for men and women.[17] The principle of sex equality is one that has largely been established as a given.

Some believe that Phyllis Schlafly was a "front"—that behind her were the interests of insurance companies and other economic interests that opposed the ERA as a financial cost to them to be avoided. Both the United States Chambers of Commerce and the National Association of Manufacturers opposed the ERA. Now, to some degree, the Affordable Care Act has eliminated the discrimination against women that was embedded in insurance industry rates and practices, but only in the context of health insurance. Sex discrimination persists in pricing, wages, hiring, and pensions, just to name a few vitally important financial concerns for women. Most, though not all, explicitly discriminatory laws have been changed in past decades, yet discrimination against women in law also persists in various ways. The adverse impact on women of laws that are seemingly neutral has been well documented but not effectively addressed. We know that women are not yet really equal, whether it is the oft-cited 77 cents earned by women for every dollar earned by men, or the failure of the police to provide women with equal protection of the law as a matter of right in the context of domestic violence.

While many have looked to the Fourteenth Amendment for a remedy for sex discrimination, effective relief has been greatly limited by the way in which the Supreme Court has interpreted it. The Fourteenth Amendment was adopted in 1868 following the Civil War. It was intended to address racial discrimination in the aftermath of slavery by prohibiting states from denying any person "the equal protection of the laws." Yet it was not until the Nineteenth Amendment was ratified in 1920 that women even had the right to vote, and it was only in 1971—more than a century after the Fourteenth Amendment came into effect—that the Supreme Court for the first time struck down a law under the Equal Protection Clause of this amendment because the law discriminated on the basis of sex. Moreover, the Fourteenth Amendment has been limited virtually from its beginning to state action by government and public officials, while so often sex and race discrimination result from private action by individuals. To the extent that there is federal legal protection from private acts of discrimination by employers and others, it is not constitutionally based on the Fourteenth Amendment.

And to this day, the Supreme Court uses a different and lower standard of review for sex discrimination claims under the Fourteenth Amendment than it does for claims of racial or religious discrimination. While racial and religious discrimination are subject to "strict scrutiny," sex discrimination is subject to the lower standard of "intermediate scrutiny." This means that for cases involving racial or religious discrimination, the courts will look to see whether the law under challenge is *necessary* to achieve a *compelling* governmental interest, while for cases involving sex discrimination, the courts will look to see whether the law under challenge bears a *substantial relationship* to an *important* governmental interest. The governmental interest need not be "compelling," and the law that furthers this interest need not be "necessary." It's ironic, and telling, that the Supreme Court, in enforcing equal protection of the law under the Constitution, does so in a discriminatory manner, holding those who would discriminate on the basis of sex accountable to a lower standard than those who would discriminate on the basis of race or religion.

Even if the Supreme Court were to heighten its standard of review for sex discrimination cases, the Fourteenth Amendment would not be effective in addressing discrimination against women for other reasons. In 1974, the Supreme Court ruled that discrimination against pregnant women did not constitute sex discrimination, although the court recognized that only women could get pregnant. The court found that the exclusion of pregnant women from employment insurance benefits available to others unable to work temporarily did not constitute discrimination against women, disregarding the disparate impact this exclusion has on women.

More generally, systemic bias has not been considered by the Supreme Court to violate the equal protection guarantee of the Fourteenth

Amendment unless the bias can be shown to have been intentional. This intent requirement leaves women with no legal recourse under the Fourteenth Amendment for many forms of discrimination, including unequal pay for equal work. Indifference to inequality and subconscious bias have had the same or even more harmful impact on women as intentional discrimination, but the Fourteenth Amendment has not effectively addressed this harm.

The courts have also failed to give women equal protection under the Constitution from discrimination by the police and other agents of law enforcement in responding to violence, leading at times to injuries and even fatalities that might have been avoided if the violence had been taken more seriously, as a violation of constitutional rights. And even though the Fourteenth Amendment guarantees equal protection of the laws, the Supreme Court has upheld a law that treats unmarried men and women citizens differently when it comes to granting citizenship to their children born outside the country.

Without effective constitutional protection from the Fourteenth Amendment for many forms of sex discrimination, and in the absence of an ERA, targeted federal legislation has been used to try to close the gaps, generally relying on the Commerce Clause of the Constitution. The Equal Pay Act of 1963; Title VII of the Civil Rights Act of 1964, which prohibits employment discrimination by employers with fifteen or more employees; Title IX of the Education Amendments of 1972, which prohibits sex discrimination in federally funded educational programs; the Pregnancy Discrimination Act of 1978; and the Violence Against Women Act of 1994 are just a few of these laws. While they have significantly helped women, these federal laws are not comprehensive, many are not fully inclusive, and one has been partially struck down by the Supreme Court for lack of a constitutional foundation. Most critically, none of these laws has the force of a constitutional amendment. That means they do not cover everyone and they can be rolled back at any time by a simple congressional vote. While the process of amending the Constitution is much longer and more complicated than the passage of federal legislation, in the long run the Equal Rights Amendment is a quicker and easier fix than trying to get Congress to pass and the courts to enforce specific legislation addressing each and every form of sex discrimination in the workplace, in schools, at home, and in the community.

In addition to simplicity and efficiency, the Equal Rights Amendment is also an important statement of principle that is much needed in the ongoing effort to move toward meaningful equality between women and men. The law is a formal expression of public policy that plays a critical role in advancing social norms. Laws articulate what we consider to be right and wrong, and can regulate, as well as influence, social conduct. Beyond the value of litigation in providing much-needed access to remedies for women who are discriminated against on the basis of sex, an Equal Rights Amendment will promote public understanding that all men and women are created free and equal in dignity and in rights, and should be treated as such.

Historically women have been treated as second-class citizens, in the United States and around the world—economically, socially, and politically as well as legally. Increasingly, as the women's movement has grown in strength, governments have recognized and tried to address this discrimination. Yet, to the surprise of many Americans, the United States is one of only seven countries in the world (along with Iran, Somalia, Sudan, South Sudan, and two small Pacific Island nations, Palau and Tonga) that have not ratified the United Nations Convention on the Elimination of All Forms of Discrimination Against Women (CEDAW). Known as the international bill of rights for women, CEDAW has been signed and ratified by 187 countries—virtually every country in the world except ours.

Ratification of CEDAW has not resulted immediately in sex equality in these 187 countries. However, it has given women and men in these countries a declaration of principle and a framework for legal action to translate this principle into practice. The failure of the United States to ratify CEDAW has made it particularly difficult for American women's rights activists to advocate effectively for action in other countries to strengthen the law and implementation of women's rights.

CEDAW was signed by President Jimmy Carter in 1980, more than thirty years ago, but it must be ratified by a two-thirds vote of the Senate to enter into force. In their ongoing effort to get the United States Senate to ratify CEDAW, women's rights advocates have often been told that CEDAW would be a "back door" to the ERA because it prohibits discrimination on the basis of sex, and as a treaty under the Supremacy Clause of the Constitution, it would be considered the law of the land, protecting citizens in all states. While this has always seemed a more compelling argument for rather than against CEDAW, it is high time to go through the front door with the ERA and join the more than 139 countries in the world that have sex equality provisions in their constitutions and/or prohibitions of discrimination on the basis of sex.[18]

Eleanor Roosevelt chaired the United Nations Human Rights Commission that drafted the Universal Declaration of Human Rights, which was adopted in 1948 and which she considered one of her greatest accomplishments. She realized, though, that human rights go from local to global:

> Where, after all, do universal human rights begin? In small places, close to home—so close and so small that they cannot be seen on any maps of the world. Yet they are the world of the individual person; the neighborhood he lives in; the school or college he attends; the factory, farm, or office where he works. Such are the places where every man, woman, and child seeks equal justice, equal opportunity, equal dignity without discrimination. Unless these rights have meaning there, they have little meaning anywhere. Without concerted citizen action to uphold them close to home, we shall look in vain for progress in the larger world.[19]

We cannot hope for our country to be a true global leader on women's rights when we lack legal recognition of women's equality rights, not only in our international legal commitments but even in our own Constitution.

Last but not least, why now? With so many pressing policy priorities and such a challenging political climate in which to get any legislation passed, is it foolish to think that this is a good time to regenerate the campaign for the Equal Rights Amendment and try to cross the finish line? No, and here is why it makes sense:

First, the ERA is and should be a truly bipartisan issue. Although often now seen as a Democratic Party issue, it was a Republican, Alice Paul, who first drafted the ERA in 1923 and the amendment was first supported in a party platform by the Republican Party. To highlight a common core value of fundamental human rights and be able to move it forward despite the gridlock elsewhere would help restore faith in our legislators and give them a chance to demonstrate their commitment to equality and justice for women across party lines.

Second, the ERA is and should be an issue for men as well as women, both having much to gain from greater equality between them. Old stereotypes are quickly being replaced by new challenges as men increasingly play a greater role at home and women increasingly play a greater role in the workplace. The law needs to catch up with this evolution, at a time when the ugly male chauvinism demonstrated by the opposition to the ERA in the 1970s has been replaced by welcome male enthusiasm for the ERA and deeper understanding that sex equality is good for men as well as women and families.

Third, the passage of state equal rights amendments by almost half of the states in our federal union has demonstrated that there is nothing apocalyptic about the ERA. The more than 139 countries around the world that have made some provision for sex equality in their constitutions have shown the same. To varying degrees, state amendments have succeeded in advancing sex equality beyond what the Fourteenth Amendment has been able to achieve. Meanwhile, as interpreted by the Supreme Court, the Fourteenth Amendment has blocked efforts to advance sex equality as much as it has promoted them, underscoring the need for an Equal Rights Amendment to the Constitution that will benefit women and men in all states.

Fourth, a new generation of young women and men who have little or no patience for inequality are ready to lead the charge for the ERA. They can benefit from, and build on the experience and wisdom of, the veteran activists who gave a decade of their lives to this cause from 1972 to 1982, and who hope to see it succeed in their lifetime. The new generation of ERA supporters brings youthful energy, fresh perspective, social media skills, and a renewed sense of urgency drawn from their impatience with the slow pace of progress—all of which make the movement for the ERA unstoppable.

This book, primarily through cases that have shaped the law as it is today, highlights women who have marshaled the courage to challenge sex discrimination they have faced in their lives. Their cases show how the law has failed to deliver them justice, and how it has undermined rather than strengthened efforts to remedy sex discrimination. Hopefully, you will come to understand why we need the ERA and you will join the growing effort to put equal rights into the Constitution, once and for all. It is long overdue.

(Nicole Hollander)

# PAY INEQUITY

*I'm just not one to quit. . . . I want justice for every woman past and present that has been discriminated against . . . I brought this case because I believe that there was a pattern of discrimination at Walmart, not just in my store, but I believe it is across the country.*[1]

—Betty Dukes

Betty Dukes, lead plaintiff in a class action lawsuit against Walmart for sex discrimination in salaries and promotions. (Farmani Gallery)

Betty Dukes was the lead plaintiff in a class action against Walmart that was dismissed by the Supreme Court. Title VII of the Civil Rights Act prohibits sex discrimination in employment, but not the kind of sex discrimination that results from gender stereotyping and a corporate culture that systematically disadvantages women. The court held that even if statistics established a pattern of lower pay and slower promotion in every one of Walmart's 3,400 stores, it would not be enough for Betty and her co-workers to bring their claim.

Title VII, which covers employees in the private sector, is beyond the scope of the Fourteenth Amendment. Under the Equal Protection Clause of the Fourteenth Amendment, it is even more difficult to seek justice for sex discrimination against public employees. The Supreme Court has said that to be held responsible, the employer must have *intended* to discriminate against the women employed. Sex discrimination in the workplace can have a real and very harmful effect without necessarily being intentional. Many corporate cultures discriminate against women, and whether or not it's a matter of official policy, the result for women is the same: less pay and a lower level on the corporate ladder.

The courts have also upheld the constitutionality of paying a woman less than her male colleagues, even though they are doing the exact same work, because the woman's salary in a prior job was less than the man's. Women can expect to earn much less than men over the course of their careers—anywhere from $700,000 to $2 million less.[2]

Many women have gone to court seeking relief from the sex discrimination they face in the terms of their employment. They have been denied justice as a result of limitations in the law and the way in which it has been interpreted. This helps explain why women still earn only 77 cents on average for every dollar men earn. **An ERA could ensure that women have an effective legal remedy for systematic pay inequity.**

If you are a young woman who has graduated from high school, you can expect to earn a total of $700,000 less over the course of your career than the young men with whom you graduated. If you are a woman graduating from college, you can expect to earn $1.2 million less than your male classmates. And if you are a young woman with an advanced degree such as law or medicine, you can expect to earn $2 million less in your lifetime than your male colleagues.[3] This is unequal, and it makes a real difference in the financial security and independence of women.

The Fourteenth Amendment has been interpreted by the Supreme Court to cover only state action, and therefore any protection it offers women from employment discrimination is limited to public employees. Since federal legislation to prohibit discrimination by private employers is beyond the scope of the Fourteenth Amendment, Congress has relied on the power it has to regulate interstate commerce under the Commerce Clause to serve as a constitutional foundation for this legislation. The Equal Pay Act was passed in 1963 to prohibit employers from paying employees differently on the basis of their sex. The law mandates equal pay for equal work "on jobs the performance of which requires equal skill, effort, and responsibility, and which are performed under similar working conditions." In 1964, Title VII of the Civil Rights Act was passed, which prohibits employment discrimination on the basis of sex as well as race, color, religion, or national origin. While the Equal Pay Act governs only compensation, Title VII prohibits discrimination with respect to "terms, conditions, or privileges of employment" as well as compensation.[4]

These laws sound good. But if more than fifty years later, women are still making only 77 cents for every dollar made by men, clearly they have not been effective in equalizing pay between women and men. Over the past decades, many employees have gone to court seeking redress for discrimination in pay on the basis of sex, only to find their claims dismissed and the law working against them rather than for them. There are a number of reasons for this failure—a combination of loopholes in and interpretations of the law that have been played out in cases and upheld by the courts as constitutional. The Equal Pay Act, for example, includes a number of defenses that employers can use to justify differences in compensation. In addition to merit, seniority, and productivity, there is a defense that allows employers to claim that "any factor other than sex" is the reason for payment of different wages for equal work. This defense is also incorporated in Title VII.

Here is how this defense stopped Lola Kouba in her effort to remedy pay inequity: In 1974, Lola went to work for Allstate Insurance Company in California, where she and other new employees received a guaranteed minimum salary, calculated on the basis of ability, education, experience, and prior salary. Because women on average make less than men, their prior salary—and accordingly the minimum salary of new agents at Allstate—was on average less for women than it was for men. Lola was paid $825 per month while her male colleagues were paid at least $1,000 per month.[5] On behalf of all female agents, Lola brought a class action against Allstate, arguing that reliance on their prior salary resulted in unequal pay and constituted unlawful discrimination on the basis of sex. Allstate argued that its reliance on the prior salaries of its employees was a "factor other than sex" and therefore a legitimate reason under the law to pay women differently than men.

The district court rejected Allstate's argument, holding that an employer could not pay men and women doing exactly the same job differently based on their immediate past salaries unless the difference resulted from a "factor other than sex." The Allstate agents were all doing the same job, and the court saw no reason other than sex for the differential in their salaries.[6] But its decision was reversed in 1982 by the Ninth Circuit Court of Appeals, which said the district court had "misconstrued" the exception in the law. While acknowledging the fear that "an employer might manipulate its use of prior salary to underpay female employees," the Ninth Circuit court concluded that the Equal Pay Act does not prohibit reliance on prior salary as a "factor other than sex." The court accepted Allstate's explanation that it was using the prior salary as part of a sales-incentive program to motivate its employees to exceed the monthly minimum through sales commissions. If the monthly minimum was much greater than an employee's prior salary, the employee might be content with the minimum and would not work as hard for the extra commissions. This could be a "legitimate business reason" for the difference in salary, the Ninth Circuit court held, and therefore it was not a prohibited form of sex discrimination.[7]

In the course of further legal proceedings the case was settled, and in 1984 Allstate announced that, in its new marketing program, "all sales agent trainees and agents within the same market area will receive the same guarantee at the start of their careers." Allstate agreed to pay $5 million to more than three thousand women who had been employed as sales agents or trainees, but the company insisted that it had not discriminated in the past by using prior salary as one of the factors in determining the guaranteed starting salary of its employees.[8] This statement was consistent with the decision of the Ninth Circuit court, which set a precedent that has been relied on to deny women legal recourse for lower starting salaries.

What the *Kouba* decision means is that a woman who was paid less than a man in her last job can, for that reason, be given a lower salary than a man in her new job even though they are doing exactly the same work. Employers can continue paying women less than men because other employers have paid women less than men, without violating the Equal Pay Act or Title VII of the Civil Rights Act. By allowing payment of a differential salary based on "any factor other than sex," the law enabled Allstate to pay women less than men for the same work, disregarding—and in fact institutionalizing—past sex discrimination resulting in present wage differences based on sex. In other words, if you are getting paid less than a man for doing the same work, the fact that you have always been getting paid less than a man for doing the same work will bar you from recourse under the law for this pay disparity. It is easy to see how this kind of logic could lead to the statistics cited earlier, leaving women up to $2 million behind their male colleagues.

In 1971, the Supreme Court recognized that seemingly neutral requirements could constitute "artificial, arbitrary, and unnecessary barriers to employment . . . [that] operate invidiously to discriminate on the basis of racial or other impermissible classification." [9] In *Griggs v. Duke Power Co.*, a case challenging racial discrimination, the company had had an explicitly discriminatory policy restricting black workers to one department, which had the lowest paying positions. After passage of the Civil Rights Act, the company had removed this racist restriction but added several job requirements that led to a lower selection rate of black employees. The Supreme Court found that these requirements were unrelated to job performance and not a matter of business necessity, and as such were prohibited by Title VII. [10] In passing Title VII, said the court, Congress intended to address *all* unnecessary employment practices that led to disparity on the basis of race, sex, and other protected classifications. Unless there was a legitimate reason for any job requirement that resulted in this outcome, the requirement was seen as problematic and a violation of Title VII, regardless of the underlying intent.

However, in 1976, the Supreme Court chose not to apply the same logic to the Equal Protection Clause of the Fourteenth Amendment, making it much more difficult for victims of discrimination by government employers to prove their cases in court under the Constitution. In *Washington v. Davis*, also a racial discrimination case, the Supreme Court held that seemingly neutral policies leading to disparate impact were not unconstitutional solely because they had this disparate *impact*. Establishment of *intent* to discriminate was required to constitute a violation of equal protection of the laws under the Constitution. [11] Writing for the majority, Justice Byron White distinguished the Title VII legislation, which applies to private employers, from the Equal Protection Clause standard for government employers. He said, "We have never held that the constitutional standard for adjudicating claims of invidious racial discrimination is identical to the standards applicable under Title VII, and we decline to do so today." [12]

In effect, through its holding in *Washington*, the Supreme Court created a higher standard for constitutional claims, making it more difficult to prove discrimination as a violation of the Constitution than as a violation of Title VII. The upshot is that the government holds itself less accountable for disparate impact than it holds private employers. *Washington v. Davis* made a distinction between constitutional claims and Title VII claims, even though the employment discrimination issues are the same for the people who are discriminated against. In *Washington,* the Supreme Court could have simply applied its interpretation of Title VII to the claims brought under the Fourteenth Amendment. Instead it articulated a new, higher standard, requiring the establishment of an *intent* to discriminate for these claims against government employers.

Title VII, as interpreted by the Supreme Court in *Griggs,* envisioned disparate impact as a pattern evidencing discrimination to be remedied, barring a job-related explanation for the pattern relating to "business necessity." As the jurisprudence evolved, however, it became more and more difficult for plaintiffs to prove their cases in court. In 1989, the Supreme Court adjudicated a Title VII case from Alaska in which unskilled workers in a salmon cannery were predominantly nonwhite Filipinos and Alaskan natives while skilled workers in the "non-cannery jobs" were mostly white. Additionally, housing and dining facilities at the cannery were segregated. The plaintiffs charged their employers with using employment practices that led to the racial disparities in the workforce, such as failure to advertise openings and nepotism in hiring. In this case, *Ward's Cove Packing v. Antonio,* the Supreme Court significantly narrowed the Title VII decision it had made in *Griggs.* The court ruled that statistical disparity alone was not enough to make a case of discrimination without identifying specific employment practices causing the disparity, although it recognized that this might be considered "unduly burdensome" on plaintiffs.[13] The court also altered the burden of proof on the issue of whether such disparate racial patterns were justified by "business necessity." The court held that in their defense, employers had only to assert such a business necessity, not to prove it.

Writing for the dissent in *Ward's Cove,* a 5–4 decision, Justice John Paul Stevens called the decision "most disturbing" and recalled that the issue is "whether an employment practice has a significant adverse effect on an identifiable class of workers—regardless of the cause or motive for the practice."[14] Justice Stevens cited the specific employment practices at issue, such as nepotism in hiring, as "obvious barriers to employment opportunities for nonwhites" and characterized the segregation of housing and dining and the stratification of jobs along racial lines as bearing "an unsettling resemblance to aspects of a plantation economy." [15]

Following the *Ward's Cove* case, in 1991, Congress amended Title VII "to respond to recent decisions of the Supreme Court by expanding the scope of relevant civil rights statutes in order to provide adequate protection to victims of discrimination." The law provided explicitly that an employee could prove a case of sex discrimination by showing that an employment practice resulted in a disparate impact on the basis of sex, when the employer failed to show that the practice "is required by business necessity." [16] This amendment effectively reinstated the law as it had been interpreted in the *Griggs* decision. Despite this clarification of "disparate impact" by Congress, however, the Supreme Court has continued to make it very difficult for employees to make claims of sex discrimination under Title VII, as evidenced by the Walmart case, in which the court narrowly interpreted the nature of discriminatory employment practices for which an employer could be held accountable.

In 1994, Betty Dukes went to work for Walmart in California as a cashier making $5 per hour. Walmart is the largest private employer in the United States, and Betty wanted to climb the corporate ladder. She made it to the level of customer service manager after three years, but advancing became more and more difficult. In 2001, Betty and five other women sued Walmart in a class action lawsuit on behalf of 1.5 million women who were working or had worked in a Walmart store since 1998. The women charged Walmart with violating Title VII by paying its male employees more than its female employees for the same work and by promoting men faster and further than women.

The case went all the way to the Supreme Court, but the issue was not whether Walmart paid men more than women, or promoted men faster than women. The issue was whether Betty Dukes could bring a lawsuit under Title VII on behalf of all the women who worked in a Walmart store. To sustain a class action lawsuit, those in the class who wish to bring a collective lawsuit must raise questions of law or fact that are common to the class. In 2004, the district court ruled that the group of women who had worked in Walmart could be certified as a class for the purpose of a class action lawsuit.[17] Walmart appealed, and in 2010, the Ninth Circuit Court of Appeals affirmed the district court's decision.[18] Walmart appealed again to the highest court, and, in 2011—after ten years of litigation—the Supreme Court ruled that Betty Dukes and other women who worked at Walmart could not bring an action as a collective group against the company to address the disparate impact of its salary and promotion practices on women.[19] Even if their allegations were all taken to be true, the court held, they still would not have established a common claim of sex discrimination because there was no single identified practice directed by the company that produced the disparate employment outcome for women. Consequently, the case never went to trial.[20]

Although Walmart raised Betty's pay to $15.23 an hour once the lawsuit and related media attention started to grow, Betty—an ordained Baptist minister—told a journalist, "I'm just not one to quit . . . I want justice for every woman past and present that has been discriminated against."[21] In another interview, Betty explained, "I brought this case because I believe that there was a pattern of discrimination at Walmart, not just in my store, but I believe it is across the country." In the same interview, Walmart manager Stephanie Odle, another of the original plaintiffs in the class action lawsuit, was asked about what is called at the top corporate level of Walmart "the Walmart way"—a culture that allows discrimination against women to flourish, according to one of the expert witnesses in the case. Stephanie, who over the course of eight years worked in nine Walmart stores in three different states, confirmed that "the Walmart way" favors men over women. She recalled a conversation with one store's district manager in which she inadvertently found out that one of her male colleagues was making $10,000 more a year than she was. The district manager explained to her, "He has a wife and kids to support." In another conversation with a general manager, she asked for a raise on behalf of two women working for her who she felt were extremely underpaid; the general manager replied, "Oh, those girls make enough money. They don't need another raise."[22]

Walmart did not have an express policy of discrimination. The claim made by the women employees was that local supervisors and store managers were given discretion to make salary and promotion decisions, and these decisions were being made in a manner that discriminated against women, in accordance with the corporate culture of Walmart. The Walmart women claimed that "the Walmart way" allowed gender-biased stereotypes to affect the decisions made over salary and promotion and that Walmart did nothing to control the local discretion that produced these results. Clearly the corporate culture had a disparate impact. The women presented statistical evidence about disparity between male and female employees in pay and promotion by the company, anecdotal reports of discrimination from more than one hundred female employees, and expert testimony from a sociologist who analyzed the culture and corporate practices of Walmart.

According to Justice Antonin Scalia, who wrote the Walmart decision for the Supreme Court, this evidence was "worlds away" from the proof required to establish that Walmart "operated under a general policy of discrimination." [23] He noted that *even if* the statistical evidence established a pattern of lower pay and slower promotion for women in *all* of Walmart's 3,400 stores, that would not be enough to certify the class to enable women in Walmart to move forward together with a common claim of sex discrimination in a class action. He suggested they had nothing in common except being women and working for Walmart. In fact, these were the common elements that led to pay inequity, and four of the Supreme Court Justices dissented from the court's judgment, including the three women justices on the court. In the dissent, Justice Ginsburg supported the conclusions of the lower courts that in this case there were questions of law or fact common to the class, as required for its certification. She identified the common question as "whether Wal-Mart's pay and promotion policies gave rise to unlawful discrimination," and commented:

> The practice of delegating to supervisors large discretion to make personnel decisions, uncontrolled by formal standards, has long been known to have the potential to produce disparate effects. Managers, like all humankind, may be prey to biases, of which they are unaware. The risk of discrimination is heightened when those managers are predominantly of one sex, and

are steeped in a corporate culture that perpetuates gender stereotypes.[24]

Sex discrimination in the workplace can have a real and very harmful effect without necessarily being intentional. Subconsciously, employers may, and often do, act in a way that perpetuates the second-class status of women as a group, leading to less favorable terms and conditions of work, including salary and promotion. Often women's work is not valued. Anytime there is a pattern of lower pay and slower promotion for women, there is no question that women will be disadvantaged by that pattern. The law, as interpreted by the Supreme Court, has denied women an effective legal remedy for this disadvantage by making it "unduly burdensome" for plaintiffs such as Betty Dukes and all the women with whom she brought legal action against Walmart. If in every Walmart store women are paid and promoted less, and if the Supreme Court accepts that this might be the case yet still finds that nothing can be done about it as a whole, then it is easy to imagine that women in Walmart stores will continue to be paid and promoted less. Many corporate cultures discriminate against women, and whether or not it's a matter of official policy, the result for women is the same: less pay and a lower level on the corporate ladder.

Even successful lawsuits under current legislation, as narrowly interpreted by the courts, have not readily secured justice for women challenging pay inequity. While Betty Dukes was working at Walmart, Lilly Ledbetter was working at Goodyear Tire and Rubber Company in Alabama. When Lilly started working for Goodyear in 1979, she received the same wages as male employees, but by the time of her retirement almost twenty years later, she was earning significantly less than her male co-workers. In November 1998, after her retirement, Lilly sued Goodyear for wage discrimination under Title VII and the Equal Pay Act. At trial, the jury found that Lilly Ledbetter had been evaluated unfairly because of her sex and for that reason had been paid significantly less than her male co-workers. She was awarded back pay and damages. Goodyear appealed, arguing that the 180-day statute of limitations barred most of her claims.

The Eleventh Circuit Court of Appeals agreed with Goodyear and reversed the district court's judgment, ruling that Lilly Ledbetter could claim for damages based only on paychecks received no more than 180 days before she commenced legal action.[25] In 2007, the Supreme Court upheld the Eleventh Circuit court's decision, citing a prior case in which Justice Stevens had held that a discriminatory act falling outside the statute of limitations was "merely an unfortunate event in history which has no present legal consequences." [26] Lilly had worked for almost twenty years at Goodyear, but under the court's decision, she could be compensated at most for only the last six months of her employment. After the decision was rendered, the Lilly Ledbetter Fair Pay Act was introduced in Congress. This bill was brought in response to the case, to revise the law to ensure that prior acts of pay discrimination outside of the 180-day statute of limitations could be incorporated into claims if the discrimination was continuing. The law passed in January 2009, providing that the statute of limitations for these claims resets with each paycheck resulting from discriminatory action. Court-awarded compensation and punitive damages are still subject to a cap, however, under Title VII.

These cases have addressed, or more often failed to address, pay inequity between men and women doing the same job in the same workplace. Women as a class also face discrimination in the economy as a whole. For example, more than 75 percent of all truck drivers in 2009 were men, while more than 75 percent of all nursing aides were women. And while the average weekly earnings of truck drivers was $685 in 2009, the average weekly earnings of nursing aides was $438.[27] Driving a truck is not the same job as being a nursing aide. However, in terms of the job characteristics enumerated in the Equal Pay Act—skill, effort, and responsibility—comparisons can be made. The fact that those—mostly women—who are paid to take care of children earn less than janitors and those who are paid to park cars[28] is clearly not an indicator of the skill, effort, and responsibility required to care for children. It is evidence of sex discrimination against jobs regarded as "women's work."

While the Equal Pay Act is limited to jobs within the same workplace, Title VII does not have this limitation in its language. In 1981, four female prison guards sued the County of Washington in Oregon under Title VII for paying them less than male prison guards. Although the male guards worked in a different prison, where they were each responsible for more prisoners, the Supreme Court recognized that the protections under Title VII of the Civil Rights Act were broader than those of the Equal Pay Act, which only addressed compensation for "equal work." The issue in this case, *County of Washington v. Gunther*, was not that the men got paid more for equal work but that, unlike their female counterparts, they got paid 100 percent of the evaluated worth of their jobs, as determined by an evaluation commissioned by the county. The same evaluation determined that the female guards should be paid 95 percent as much as the male guards, but instead of 95 percent, the county decided to pay female guards only 70 percent as much as the male guards.[29]

The Supreme Court clarified in this case that claims of wage discrimination brought under Title VII were not limited to equal pay for the exact same work, as they are under the Equal Pay Act. The discrimination recognized by the court was the disproportionate reduction in pay for the value of the work done by female guards, as compared with the full pay to male guards for the value of the work they did. The County of Washington's intent to discriminate was clear from the decision to pay female guards less than the amount recommended while paying male guards the full amount recommended. In light of this decision, it seemed possible that Title VII, unlike the Equal Pay Act, could be an avenue of recourse for women who were not getting paid equally for work of comparable worth.

In 1974 the Iowa State Board of Regents introduced a system of compensation that was designed to evaluate each job's worth objectively and establish internal equity among university jobs. The system was created to eliminate the disparity against those in job categories dominated by women. At the University of Northern Iowa, all clerical employees were women, while the majority of employees working in the physical plant were men. However, the local job market paid higher wages for physical plant jobs than it did for clerical jobs, and so the starting salary for physical plant jobs at the university was below market. To address this, the university started its physical plant employees at a more senior level in the system so that their salaries would be competitive with the market. Consequently, the university paid physical plant employees, mostly men, more than clerical employees, all women, for jobs that had been assessed as being at the same labor grade. The clerical employees sued the university for maintaining this wage disparity as sex discrimination violating Title VII of the Civil Rights Act. The district court, affirmed by the Tenth Circuit Court of Appeals, dismissed the claim, noting that physical plant jobs were open equally to male and female applicants and holding that there was no intention in passing Title VII to interfere with the market and "abrogate the laws of supply and demand or other economic principles that determine wage rates for various kinds of work."[30] In other words, if market forces discriminate against women by paying them less for jobs of comparable worth, the courts will not intervene, and the discrimination will continue.

In 1982, the American Federation of State, County, and Municipal Employees (AFSCME) sued the state of Washington in a class action lawsuit on behalf of state employees working in job categories that were occupied at least 70 percent by women. The state of Washington's study of wage disparity between men and women had evaluated jobs on the basis of knowledge and skills, mental demands, accountability, and working conditions, assigning points to each category. A wage disparity of 20 percent was documented between job categories in which women predominated by 70 percent compared with job categories in which men predominated by 70 percent. The district court found that the failure of Washington State to adopt and implement a remedial program to equalize this disparity in compensation constituted sex discrimination under Title VII of the Civil Rights Act.[31] The Ninth Circuit Court of Appeals reversed, recalling that "liability for disparate treatment hinges upon proof of discriminatory intent," and noting the "failure by AFSCME to establish the requisite element of intent by either circumstantial or direct evidence."[32] In the Ninth Circuit court decision, Judge Anthony Kennedy—since elevated to the Supreme Court—expressed great concern about interfering with the free market:

> The State of Washington's initial reliance on a free market system in which employees in male-dominated jobs are

compensated at a higher rate than employees in dissimilar female-dominated jobs is not in and of itself a violation of Title VII, notwithstanding that the Willis study deemed the positions of comparable worth. Absent a showing of discriminatory motive, which has not been made here, the law does not permit the federal courts to interfere in the market-based system for the compensation of Washington's employees.[33]

In a similar prior case from Denver, Colorado, seeking to address underpayment of nurses, a female-dominated profession, the Tenth Circuit Court of Appeals in 1980 held that with regard to pay differentials between nurses and other male-dominated professions, such as real estate appraisers, "This type of disparity was not sought to be adjusted by the Civil Rights Act, and is not within the equal protection clause."[34] In the district court decision, which the Tenth Circuit court affirmed, Judge Fred M. Winner was outspoken in his acknowledgment of past discrimination and his view of the lack of congressional purpose to remedy it: "[W]hat we are confronted with here today is history . . . which I have no hesitancy at all in finding has discriminated unfairly and improperly against women. But Congress did not, in my judgment, decide that we were going to roll aside all history and that the Federal Courts should take over the job of leveling out centuries of discrimination."[35]

Canada has a federal pay equity statute as well as comparable worth programs in Quebec, Manitoba, and Ontario. The European Union Council of Ministers adopted an Equal Pay Directive in 1975 providing that equal pay means "for the same work or for work to which equal value is attributed."[36] The Swiss constitution was amended in 1981 to include similar language, and the United Kingdom, Sweden, and Australia all have legislation providing for equal pay for work of comparable worth.[37] Here in the United States, while the case law limiting legal recourse for pay inequity goes back to the 1970s, women are still going to court forty years later, determined to seek justice for the pay inequity in their work lives but unable to find it in the current federal legal framework.

In 2013, Tracy Rexroat joined the long list of women before her who

sought and were denied justice for pay inequity. In 2007, Tracy was
hired to work for the Arizona Department of Education as an education program specialist. Her starting salary was more than $17,000
lower than her male peers' when she was hired, and it remained well
below theirs three years later in 2010. Tracy sued the Department of
Education for pay discrimination, in part on the basis of the discrep-
ancy in starting salaries. The district court in Arizona relied on the
1982 *Kouba v. Allstate* case, described earlier, to remind Tracy that unequal starting salaries "do not violate the Equal Pay Act . . . as long as
there was 'an acceptable business reason' for basing wages on prior
salary. . . ."[38] Regardless of Tracy's actual prior experience, her prior
salary was used as a measure of experience, which has been deemed by
the courts to be "an acceptable business reason" for gender pay disparity rather than a manifestation of sex discrimination.

"Equal means equal" *means* that if there are systemic indicators
that women are paid less than men, there should be an effective legal
remedy to address this inequality. Whether intentional or not, pay inequity is harmful to women and constitutes discrimination based on
their sex. Title VII was clearly intended to address disparate impact,
regardless of intent, recognizing that the real problem was disparate
impact that results in unequal treatment of men and women regardless of whether it is intentional. But the Supreme Court has made it
clear that disparate impact is only a violation of constitutional rights
under the Fourteenth Amendment if it is intentional, and the courts
have made it clear that they do not want to interfere with market forces,
even if these market forces preserve the status quo. But the status
quo is what needs to change if women and men are to be equal in the
workplace.

What is missing from the Fourteenth Amendment as it has been
interpreted by the courts is a results-based approach to gender equality. Starting with the inequality that has been statistically documented
between the salaries of women and the salaries of men, the courts have
blocked efforts to address the root causes of this discrimination. By
allowing prior salaries, which incorporate and reflect the history of discrimination against women, to be used as a basis for differentiating

current salaries, the law ensures that the difference carries forward. By shielding market forces, which also reflect the lesser value that has been given to women in the workplace, the law ensures that market forces continue to reflect the pay inequity that they have historically reflected.

The Paycheck Fairness Act was reintroduced in Congress for the third time in 2013, co-sponsored by Senator Barbara Mikulski from Maryland and Representative Rosa DeLauro from Connecticut.[39] If passed, this act would amend the Equal Pay Act to allow for additional remedies, such as punitive damages against employers who discriminate. It would facilitate class action lawsuits and prohibit employer retaliation for sharing salary information. It would also limit the defense that a wage differential is based on "any factor other than sex" to bona fide factors such as education, training, or experience. However, in April 2014, the bill was blocked in the Senate by a vote of 54 to 43.

The courts have explicitly stated that it is not for them to "roll aside all history" and to "take over the job of leveling out centuries of discrimination." An Equal Rights Amendment to the Constitution with the purpose of remedying discrimination could make it their job to *change* history and end sex discrimination rather than facilitating its continuity. An Equal Rights Amendment could have been used to invalidate the reliance by Allstate Insurance Company on prior salaries as a "factor other than sex" to start Lola Kouba at a lower salary than her male colleagues. An Equal Rights Amendment could have been used to enable Betty Dukes to challenge the systematic disparity between women and men in their pay and promotion by Walmart without having to prove that there was an explicit corporate policy in place to create this disparity. And an Equal Rights Amendment could have been used to ensure that women working for the Iowa State Board of Regents as clerical employees were paid the same as men working for Iowa State as physical plant employees.

It is inherently unfair to perpetuate the relatively lower starting salaries of women, to pay women less and promote them more slowly, and to value the work that women do less than the work that men do when the same level of knowledge, skills, and responsibility are required. An

ERA setting forth the principle of sex equality may not end this in-justice immediately, but it will offer women a more effective avenue of legal recourse. This could make a meaningful difference in the power of the law to bring real equality between women and men to the workplace.

# PREGNANCY DISCRIMINATION

*And he pretty much said, you're too much of a liability in our building; don't come back until you're no longer pregnant. I just kind of looked at him like, are you serious? Like, I can't work? And he was like, no—[he] wouldn't let me.*[1]

—Peggy Young

Peggy Young brought a lawsuit against UPS for pregnancy discrimination. (Sharon Gustofson)

Peggy Young sued United Parcel Service (UPS) when they refused to let her work during her pregnancy. The Supreme Court ruled in 1976 that pregnancy discrimination is *not* sex discrimination under the Constitution. The Pregnancy Discrimination Act subsequently passed by Congress affirmed that pregnancy discrimination *is* sex discrimination under Title VII of the Civil Rights Act, but in Peggy's case the court described the UPS policy as "pregnancy blind," finding it nondiscriminatory because it treated pregnant employees the same as nonpregnant employees. Her appeal is currently pending before the Supreme Court.

*I had no money. I had no job. I had no car. I was job hunting by bus, with her in my arms. . . . Women should not have to choose between having a job and having a baby.*[2]

—Lillian Garland

Lillian Garland sued California Federal Savings & Loan Association for giving her job to someone else while she was on pregnancy leave. The company argued that giving a pregnant woman the right to job reinstatement, as California law did, violated Title VII of the Civil Rights Act by giving her *more* rights than men, while Title VII required *equal* rights. The Supreme Court upheld the California law, but it is a state law that protects women only in California. The courts have said women have no right to "preferential treatment" as a result of pregnancy. The presumption is that a worker is someone who does not become pregnant, and this creates an adversity in the workplace for women who become pregnant, while men face no comparable adversity. Accommodating pregnancy is equal treatment. Lillian recalled her day in court: "I walked over to the girls, teen-age girls, and introduced myself, and I said: 'I am fighting for you, I am fighting so you will be able to one day, if you decide to get married and have a family, you'll be able to keep your job if you want to have a baby,' and a little girl looked at me and said: 'Thank you.'"[3]

**The ERA could create a right to sex equality that in the context of pregnancy recognizes that women and men have equal rights to work and have children at the same time.**

Natasha Jackson was the only woman working at a Rent-A-Center in South Carolina, where she was an account executive when she became pregnant in 2008. The store manager congratulated her and helped her deal with morning sickness by changing her schedule, which worked better for him as well. But when the district manager learned of Natasha's pregnancy, he ordered her to go home and take a two-week paid leave. Because her doctor said she could not lift more than twenty to twenty-five pounds, which Natasha did only occasionally, she was placed on a further twelve-week unpaid leave. She was subsequently told she could not return to work until after delivering her baby and then only if her job was still available, with no guarantee that it would be. She had just made a down payment on a house, but she had to back out of the deal and lost the chance to own her own home. Two and one-half months after her baby was born, Rent-A-Center sent Natasha a letter telling her she could not return to work without a doctor's note clearing her for work without restriction. She returned with this note but was fired anyway. Natasha brought a claim against her employer for pregnancy discrimination, which went to arbitration, but after three years she lost her case.[4] "Everything from that moment in my life just took a down spiral," she said in an interview. "I never recovered."[5]

Natasha's case is recent, within the last few years. After more than forty years of legislation and litigation, women are still losing their jobs when they become pregnant and still losing their cases when they look to the courts for a legal remedy. To date, pregnancy discrimination—as incomprehensible as it may seem—is not recognized as sex discrimination under the Constitution, although there has been a sustained effort to address pregnancy discrimination through federal law. At the heart of the matter is the inherent bias of the workplace norm, which has historically been formulated by and for men who have no need to accommodate pregnancy. With a norm defined around men, rather than all people, the needs of women—unlike the needs of men—are seen as "different" rather than as normal. While some progress has been made, it is around the margins of the issue. The history of this long and ongoing effort is summarized on the following pages, demonstrating how painstakingly difficult and ultimately unsuccessful it has been, and underscoring the need for an amendment to the Constitution to clarify that pregnancy discrimination *is* a form of sex discrimination from which women should be guaranteed constitutional protection.

In 1973, the court of appeals in California drew a line between pregnancy-related complications and pregnancy itself when Gail Rentzer challenged the state disability fund for failing to compensate her for wages lost as a result of pregnancy-related complications. Gail had suffered an ectopic pregnancy that required her to have emergency surgery and left her unable to work for six weeks. She was denied compensation by the California Unemployment Insurance Appeals Board because the fund's regulations stated that the term "disability" did not include "any injury or illness caused by or arising in connection with pregnancy." Gail filed a complaint in the California state court system, challenging the company's denial of unemployment compensation to her as a violation of equal protection of the law.

The California courts had previously ruled that it was all right to exclude pregnancy from disability coverage. Giving pregnant women disability compensation would really be a "maternity benefit," the court of appeals had said in an earlier case, while "the purpose of the unemployment disability program is to afford relief to employees sustaining loss of wages on account of illness, and not to confer maternity benefits." [6] In Gail's case, the court of appeals reaffirmed this earlier decision, which allowed the exclusion of normal pregnancy, but said that it did not apply to Gail because she had not had a normal pregnancy. The court of appeals reasoned that Gail's ectopic pregnancy was not "ordinary maternity" and that the purpose of the emergency surgery she underwent was not to deliver a child but to stop the bleeding and repair the fallopian tube in which the pregnancy had occurred. Because she had not had a "true pregnancy," the court held that Gail was entitled to disability benefits for the period in which she was unable to work.[7] The disability fund guidelines in California were subsequently revised to include cases where pregnancy *complications* led to a temporary inability to work. However, inability to work due to *ordinary maternity* remained outside the scope of disability compensation.

More than six million women in the United States become pregnant every year,[8] making pregnancy on the job a common occurrence. Women who have pregnancy complications are now better protected and some progress has been made in protecting employees who have a normal pregnancy. Yet normal pregnancy can still result in the loss of a job and wages without legal remedy when pregnant employees are unable or not allowed to work as a result of the pregnancy. At the same time that Gail brought her case in a state court, Carolyn Aiello challenged this aspect of the California disability fund in federal court. Like Gail, Carolyn had suffered pregnancy complications, and when the rules were changed as a result of Gail's case, Carolyn and other women who joined her lawsuit and also had suffered pregnancy complications became eligible for benefits. However, one of the other plaintiffs in the federal case, Jacqueline Jaramillo, had claimed benefits because she was unable to work as a result of a normal pregnancy. Jacqueline had become pregnant as a result of a failed IUD. A Catholic, she was committed to childbirth, although the pregnancy was ill-timed. She was working to put her husband through school, and she applied to the state disability fund for compensation to cover the six weeks her doctor had told her to plan to be away from work following delivery.[9] The fund denied her claim, and she challenged her denial as being unconstitutional, a violation of her right to equal protection of the laws under the Fourteenth Amendment.

Initially, the district court agreed with Jacqueline that the exclusion of pregnancy from unemployment fund benefits violated her rights under the Fourteenth Amendment.[10] On appeal, however, the Supreme Court reversed this decision. The court reasoned that because it would be substantially more costly to include pregnancy, either employee contribution rates to the fund would have to be higher, benefits paid out for disabilities would have to be lower, or there would have to be a state subsidy of the fund. To date, the fund had been entirely supported by employee contributions through a formula whereby all employees paid 1 percent of their salaries, which entitled them to disability compensation for up to twenty-six weeks. The Constitution, according to the Supreme Court, could not possibly require the state of California "to subordinate or compromise its legitimate interests solely to create a more comprehensive social insurance program than it already has."[11]

The purpose of the state disability fund was to cover the losses incurred by employees as a result of their temporary inability to work for health-related reasons. Clearly an important underlying factor in the Supreme Court's decision in this California case, *Geduldig v. Aiello*, was the additional cost of covering pregnancy. But other disability benefits already available in California covered inability to work for up to twenty-six weeks, so it was not really the required amount of funding that led to the court's decision. It was the fact that this inability to work affected only women, which touched upon the inherent bias that had led to the definition of normal disability that excluded normal pregnancy. Yet if women are in the workforce, as they were in the 1970s and are even more so now, then it is inevitable that a significant number of these women will at some point become pregnant and potentially face a loss of wages as a result of their temporary inability to work. While the risks of all other disability costs were pooled in the fund, the risk of pregnancy-related costs was left to fall individually on the women who became pregnant. The cost is the same either way, and the real question is whether it is fair, and constitutional, for this particular cost uniquely affecting women in the workplace to be borne individually rather than collectively.

In discussing whether the exclusion of pregnancy from the disability fund's coverage was a form of sex discrimination, the Supreme Court reasoned that "[t]here is no risk from which men are protected and women are not. Likewise, there is no risk from which women are protected and men are not," explaining further that "while it is true that only women can become pregnant, it does not follow that every legislative classification concerning pregnancy is a sex-based classification. . . . [N]ormal pregnancy is an objectively identifiable physical condition with unique characteristics."[12] The failure to cover a risk only to women, while there was no risk only to men from which men were not protected, was held by the Supreme Court not to be a distinction based on sex. Thus the court found that it does not violate the equal protection under the laws guaranteed by the Fourteenth Amendment.

In other words, the Supreme Court held that because *men* can't get pregnant, there is no discrimination in excluding pregnancy altogether from disability coverage. This reasoning leads to the conclusion that if men are not affected by the disability, then the loss it produces does not have to be covered collectively, leaving on women alone the responsibility for the cost of pregnancy-related loss of wages. Not every disability affects every worker, but the idea of disability insurance is to protect all workers from whatever disability causes them to lose wages as a result of their inability to work. If one were to start with a sex-blind workplace and try to identify the health-related causes that would most likely lead to temporary inability to work, surely pregnancy would be high on the list.

In a compelling dissent by three Supreme Court justices, Justice William J. Brennan pointed out the fact that the state disability fund paid compensation for "virtually all disabling conditions without regard to cost, voluntariness, uniqueness, predictability, or 'normalcy' of the disability," including cosmetic surgery, sterilization, and removal of wisdom teeth. He noted that the economic effects of pregnancy are "functionally indistinguishable from the effects caused by any other disability," namely lost wages and medical expenses. In singling out pregnancy, unique to women, for less favorable treatment by the disability fund, the state of California had, Justice Brennan contended, created "a double standard for disability compensation" in which men receive full compensation for all disabilities but women do not. With simple logic, he concluded, "Such dissimilar treatment of men and women, on the basis of physical characteristics inextricably linked to one sex, inevitably constitutes sex discrimination."[13]

Of all costs that might be equally shared, pregnancy would be one that uniquely benefits both women and men, as well as society as a whole. Yet while both women and men were collectively compensated for all other nonwork-related reasons for not being able to work temporarily, the Supreme Court's decision in *Geduldig v. Aiello* left pregnant women to bear the full cost of their pregnancies alone.

Two years later, in 1976, having lost the argument that pregnancy-related discrimination violated the Fourteenth Amendment prohibition on sex discrimination, seven women from Virginia, led by Martha Gilbert, gave the Supreme Court another chance to address pregnancy-related discrimination as a violation of Title VII of the Civil Rights Act. The women brought a class action against their employer, General Electric. The company offered its employees a disability benefit that was all-inclusive, with the exception of pregnancy-related disabilities, which were excluded.

After a trial on the merits, the district court ruled in favor of the women, holding that General Electric's exclusion of pregnancy from disability benefits violated Title VII's prohibition on sex discrimination.[14] Again the Supreme Court reversed this decision, which had been affirmed by the Fourth Circuit Court of Appeals, and held that pregnancy-related discrimination did not constitute sex discrimination under Title VII. Again Justice Brennan dissented, writing, "Surely it offends common sense" to suggest that a pregnancy-related classification is not sex-related.[15]

In his dissent, Justice Brennan referred to the history of General Electric's treatment of female employees as evidence of purposeful discrimination. When it was first formulated in 1926, the benefit plan was not offered to female employees because they were thought to be hoping to get married and leave the company. In those early days, women's wages in the company were scaled at two-thirds the level of men's wages. Justice Brennan noted the company policy of forced maternity leave coupled with nonpayment of disability benefits.

While the majority decision of the Supreme Court had drawn a line between pregnancy and disability, characterizing pregnancy as a "voluntary decision," Justice Brennan pointed out that the company policy allowed disability benefits for attempted suicide, elective cosmetic surgery, and venereal disease—all just as "voluntary" or more so than pregnancy. The dissenting justice also cited some reproduction-related procedures unique to men, such as prostatectomies, vasectomies, and circumcisions, that were covered for disability benefits by General Electric while pregnancy was the only one—"sex-specific or otherwise"—that was excluded from the plan. Based on the company's policy and history, Justice Brennan rejected the notion that the disability benefits represented a "sex-neutral assignment of risks" rather than a "sex-conscious process expressive of the secondary status of women in the company's labor force." [16]

Advocacy by the women's movement prompted Congress to respond to the *Gilbert* decision, which had found for General Electric at the expense of pregnant women, by amending Title VII in 1978 through passage of the Pregnancy Discrimination Act (PDA). This law explicitly provided that the language in Title VII ("on the basis of sex") included "on the basis of pregnancy, childbirth, or related medical conditions." [17] In the same year, California also amended its Fair Employment and Housing Act (FEHA) to require employers in California to give certain benefits to pregnant employees—up to four months unpaid disability leave, and a right to job reinstatement after this leave unless the job was no longer available due to business necessity. In that case, the employer had to make a good faith effort to put the employee in a job similar to the one she had held. [18]

In January 1982, Lillian Garland took pregnancy disability leave from her job at California Federal Savings & Loan Association (Cal Fed), where she had worked as a receptionist for several years. In April, two months after her baby daughter was born by cesarean section, she was ready to go back to work. But Cal Fed told her that her job had been given to someone else and there were no similar positions available. Lillian sued Cal Fed for violating FEHA by giving her job to someone else while she was on leave. In response, Cal Fed took the position that Title VII trumped FEHA and that Title VII did not give pregnant employees a right to reinstatement. Cal Fed further argued that the FEHA right to job reinstatement for pregnant employees violated Title VII by giving women *more* rights than men, while Title VII required *equal* rights on the basis of sex.

The district court agreed with Cal Fed and dismissed the case, finding that California state laws requiring "preferential treatment of female employees disabled by pregnancy" are preempted by Title VII and are "null, void, invalid and inoperative." [19] The court's holding relied on the Supremacy Clause of the Constitution, which provides that when a conflict between state and federal law arises, federal law must prevail. The Ninth Circuit Court of Appeals reversed this ruling, holding that there was no conflict in this case between state and federal law. The court of appeals said the district court's conclusion that the California law discriminated against men on the basis of pregnancy "defies common sense, misinterprets case law, and flouts Title VII and the PDA."[20] The California legislation helping pregnant employees keep their jobs *promoted* the goal of equal employment opportunity for women, the Ninth Circuit court reasoned. It was consistent with the Pregnancy Discrimination Act, which had been adopted by Congress "to construct a floor beneath which pregnancy disability benefits may not drop—not a ceiling above which they may not rise."[21]

The Supreme Court affirmed the Ninth Circuit court's decision upholding the California law. The Supreme Court recalled that the purpose of Title VII was "to achieve equality of employment opportunities and remove barriers that have operated in the past to favor an identifiable group of . . . employees over other employees."[22] When the Pregnancy Discrimination Act had been passed, in response to the *Gilbert* case denying pregnant women the same rights as those temporarily disabled for other reasons, Congress had considered extensive evidence of pregnancy discrimination in the workplace. It intended the law to "provide relief for working women and to end discrimination against pregnant workers."[23] When the bill was debated, Representative Shirley Chisholm told Congress it "affords some 41 percent of this Nation's labor force some greater degree of protection and security without fear of reprisal due to their decision to bear children," and Representative Paul Tsongas said the bill "would put an end to an unrealistic and unfair system that forces women to choose between family and career—clearly a function of sex bias in the law."[24]

The Supreme Court understood that the California law mandating job protection for women following pregnancy leave "allows women, as well as men, to have families without losing their jobs."[25] The Pregnancy Discrimination Act passed by Congress had the same goal. While the PDA provided for equal entitlements to pregnant women without specifically naming any entitlements, the California law was designed to address the problem faced uniquely by women who were effectively being forced to choose between jobs and pregnancy, a choice men who wanted to have children were not forced to make. This was understood by California to constitute discrimination against women by denying them equal opportunity in the workplace. The law passed in California was intended to address this discrimination against women, but it was challenged as being "preferential" and discriminatory against men, although without this job protection, women undoubtedly would face additional career limitations and consequently less employment opportunity than men.

In the *Cal Fed* case, the Supreme Court allowed California to try to level the playing field. However, the Pregnancy Discrimination Act does no such thing for women in states that do not have legislation mandating job security for pregnant women. The Family and Medical Leave Act, passed by Congress in 1993, enables parents to take up to twelve weeks of unpaid leave if they have been working continuously for at least a year, but this protection applies only to those who work in companies with at least fifty employees.

While Lillian Garland's case against Cal Fed was a victory for women in California, it took a great toll on Lillian herself. She was reinstated while the case was pending, but Cal Fed did not give her back her job as a receptionist. She was asked to clean out storage rooms as well as to file and type, and she left two years later, claiming she was forced out following a *60 Minutes* television show about her case. While she was unemployed, the father of her child left her and took custody of their little girl. She didn't fight it because, as she described her life, "I had no money. I had no job. I had no car. I was job hunting by bus, with her in my arms." Despite the pain and suffering Lillian went through, she was not sorry to have brought the case. "Women should not have to choose between having a job and having a baby," she said. "But the case is over and I won. I think how many millions of women have been helped. It will affect my daughter and her daughter. It wasn't just for me."[26]

It took further litigation to establish that the Pregnancy Discrimination Act provided for equal treatment of employee spouses as well as employees. Following passage of the law, the Newport News Shipbuilding and Dry Dock Company—the largest shipbuilding company in the United States—amended its benefits plan to provide hospitalization coverage for pregnancy. Previously the plan had excluded pregnancy from coverage. However, the company did not make a similar amendment to the benefits plan for employee spouses, leaving pregnant wives of employees without the hospitalization coverage given to pregnant employees. The Fourth Circuit Court of Appeals ruled that this policy violated the act and constituted sex discrimination,[27] while in a similar case the Ninth Circuit Court of Appeals ruled that the Pregnancy Discrimination Act did not apply to spouses of male employees.[28] The Supreme Court agreed with the Fourth Circuit court and in 1983 held that providing female employees with better pregnancy benefits than the wives of male employees constituted sex discrimination against male employees.[29]

Thanks to the Pregnancy Discrimination Act, women who have normal pregnancies are now equally covered by Title VII for financial loss they sustain as a result of inability to work. In effect the law has ensured that normal pregnancy, not only pregnancy complication, is treated in the same way under Title VII as other disabilities. However, Title VII does not apply to employers with fewer than fifteen employees.[30] Moreover, unlike the Americans with Disabilities Act passed in 1990, the Pregnancy Discrimination Act and Title VII do not explicitly require employers to make "reasonable accommodation" to enable pregnant women to do the core parts of their jobs. Employees covered by the Americans with Disabilities Act cannot be fired, as pregnant women can be, for needing to take more frequent bathroom breaks or for seeking alternative work to heavy lifting. This has led to many more pregnancy discrimination cases under the Pregnancy Discrimination Act and Title VII, which to date have been largely unsuccessful.

Peggy Young worked at United Parcel Service (UPS) in Maryland for ten years. As an early morning air driver, she would meet a shuttle from the airport with letters and packages for delivery, rarely lifting more than a few pounds. When she became pregnant, her doctor recommended that she lift no more than twenty pounds. On this basis, UPS concluded that Peggy was unable to perform the essential functions of her job and also was ineligible for light-duty assignment. UPS routinely gave light-duty assignment, with ten-pound lifting restrictions, to employees who were injured on the job, as well as employees protected by the Americans with Disabilities Act for conditions such as high blood pressure, diabetes, vision or hearing problems, limb impairments, sleep apnea, and emotional problems. However, UPS had a policy of no light duty for pregnancy and refused to let Peggy work in her regular job, despite her pleas to continue. Peggy's manager told her not to come back until after her pregnancy was over. For more than six months during her pregnancy, Peggy lost her salary and benefits.

Peggy sued UPS for pregnancy discrimination, but her case was summarily dismissed by the district court, and this dismissal was upheld by the Fourth Circuit Court of Appeals, which reasoned that the Pregnancy Discrimination Act was meant only to "ensure that female workers would not be treated differently from other employees simply because of their capacity to bear children." The court described the UPS policy as "pregnancy blind," finding it nondiscriminatory because it treated pregnant employees the same as nonpregnant employees. To find otherwise, the appeals court held, "would be to "transform an antidiscrimination statute into a requirement to provide accommodation to pregnant employees, perhaps even at the expense of other, nonpregnant employees."[31] This 2013 Fourth Circuit court decision cited numerous decisions over the previous fifteen years from four other circuit courts of appeal, all holding that employers are not required by the Pregnancy Discrimination Act to assign lighter duties to employees who are unable to lift heavy loads as a result of pregnancy.[32] In these cases, the courts held again and again that denying pregnant women the alternative job assignments to which other employees with occupational injuries were entitled did not constitute a violation of the Pregnancy Discrimination Act. Despite the uniform conclusions of these circuit courts of appeal, Peggy Young has asked the Supreme Court to review the decision of the Fourth Circuit court in her case. As of this writing, her appeal is pending.[33]

Notwithstanding all the precedents denying pregnant women the right to light-duty assignment, the cases continue. Svetlana Arizanovska worked two jobs, including one as a stocker at Walmart on the overnight shift. When she became pregnant, her doctor told her not to lift more than twenty pounds. Initially Walmart put her on light duty, but soon afterward told her that no light-duty assignment was available.

She was assigned to work lifting heavy cases of food onto shelves. While doing this work, one day she started bleeding. When she told her boss, he ignored her. After finishing her shift she went to the emergency room, where she learned she had lost her baby. Four months later she became pregnant again. Even when presented with a note from her doctor saying she should not lift more than ten pounds, Walmart refused to give her a light-duty assignment. When the company tried to put her on involuntary unpaid leave, she told them she was able to work, which her doctor confirmed. However, she was not allowed back to work and was eventually fired. Soon after, she miscarried for the second time, possibly as a result of work-related stress, according to her doctor. Svetlana sued Walmart for discriminating against her during her pregnancy but lost both at the district court and on appeal in 2012, where the Seventh Circuit Court of Appeals cited the legal precedents mentioned above.[34]

In 2012, Doris Garcia was working at a Chipotle in Washington, D.C. When she became pregnant and started to use the bathroom more often, her boss yelled at her and told her she would have to get permission from him every time she needed to use the bathroom. When she started eating snacks during her fifteen-minute breaks, he stopped allowing her breaks. He also told her she was not allowed to drink water while she was working. When she asked him repeatedly for permission to leave early for a prenatal doctor's appointment, he ignored her request for several days and then threatened her on the day of the appointment with negative consequences if she left early. She went to the appointment, and the next day she was fired. For the first time in her life, Doris had to seek public assistance and live on unemployment.[35] She filed a lawsuit against Chipotle, which as of this writing is pending in a district court in Washington, D.C.[36]

The Pregnant Workers Fairness Act, introduced in Congress in 2012 and reintroduced in 2013, would require employers to provide reasonable accommodation to pregnant employees, unless doing so would impose an undue hardship. This would give pregnant employees the same level of protection that other employees have under the Americans with Disabilities Act. The bill has not passed. If it does, it would give pregnant women a better chance as well as the right to continue working during pregnancy. In denying pregnant women the right to alternative assignments with lighter lifting requirements, and allowing termination of their employment in the absence of medical clearance to work without restrictions on lifting, the courts have endorsed a workplace practice that inevitably disadvantages women.

Many women who are working when they become pregnant cannot afford to stop working. The courts have said women have no right to "preferential treatment" as a result of pregnancy, but this is not really a question of "preferential" treatment. The failure to accommodate pregnancy in the workplace is a question of discrimination, a failure to level the playing field for women who are otherwise disadvantaged by pregnancy, which can cost them their jobs without legal consequence to their employers. The presumption that a worker is someone who does not become pregnant creates an adversity in the workplace for women who become pregnant, while men do not face any comparable adversity. That presumption is clearly based on sex, yet is not recognized as such under the U.S. Constitution, and is to date not effectively remedied by legislation. This adversity results in a workplace that favors men over women, with the exception of those women who never become pregnant (and even they are vulnerable to discrimination from employers who think they *might* become pregnant).

The Supreme Court has said that pregnancy-based discrimination is not sex-based discrimination prohibited by the Fourteenth Amendment, and that remains the constitutional law of the land. Through legislation, Congress has said that pregnancy-based discrimination *is* sex-based discrimination covered by Title VII, but sex-based discrimination has been interpreted by the court as guaranteeing women rights men have, rather than guaranteeing women rights they need which have little or no correlation to what men have or need.

All people have the right to equal employment opportunity, but the case law on the Fourteenth Amendment has undermined rather than reinforced this right. When the state of California tried to reinforce this right by giving women the right they need to return to work following pregnancy, the Supreme Court allowed them to do so and recognized that giving women this right does not constitute discrimination against men. But the court has left women in other states without this right and other related rights, such as the right to reasonable accommodation of pregnancy-related needs in the workplace so that women are able to work during pregnancy. Over the past forty years, the jurisprudence of the Supreme Court has rendered the Fourteenth Amendment irrelevant to any effort to reform the legal framework for pregnancy-related employment protection. As is, this legal framework inevitably discriminates against women because they are women.

Recently, there has been a new line of attack on women's access to family planning, following the adoption of the Affordable Care Act in 2010. In 2014, legislation protecting freedom of religion was held by the Supreme Court in *Burwell v. Hobby Lobby Stores* to allow Hobby Lobby to deny the thousands of women it employs access to contraception. The court found that private companies have the right to exercise freedom of religion and that the burden to Hobby Lobby of allowing third-party insurers to provide contraceptive services to its women employees under the Affordable Care Act was "substantial."[37]

In a dissenting opinion, joined by the two other women on the Supreme Court—Justice Elena Kagan and Justice Sonia Sotomayor—as well as Justice Stephen Breyer, Justice Ginsburg assailed this decision, noting that the cost of contraceptives discourages their use by many women. In passing the Women's Health Amendment to the Affordable Care Act, Senator Dianne Feinstein had highlighted the fact that "women of childbearing age spend 68% more in out-of-pocket health costs than men."[38] Despite the grave health implications for the millions of women affected by the Hobby Lobby decision, Justice Samuel Alito made no reference to sex discrimination in writing the all-male majority opinion.

Just a few days after its decision in *Hobby Lobby*, the Supreme Court issued an emergency injunction to save Wheaton College from even having to fill out a form to send to insurance companies certifying its religious objections to contraception in order to qualify for the Affordable Care Act's exemption for religious institutions.[39] The completion of the form was found by the court to be a substantial burden on the exercise of religious freedom that would cause irreparable harm to those required to complete it. Again, the three women on the Supreme Court vehemently objected to the decision. Justices Ginsburg and Kagan joined Justice Sotomayor in a dissent pointing out its absurdity and the absence of legal justification for it.[40]

These cases are not about religious freedom. They are about sex discrimination, and they would have been decided differently if there were an Equal Rights Amendment in the Constitution. The relevant statute, the Religious Freedom Restoration Act, has been held to take precedence over the Affordable Care Act, another statute, but it could not take precedence over a provision in the Constitution. If there had been a sex equality provision in the Constitution when these cases were decided, the adverse impact on women would need to have been considered by the Court and given greater priority in its decision.

An Equal Rights Amendment could change the legal landscape by creating a right to sex equality that is fundamental and substantive. What this might mean in the context of pregnancy is recognition that women and men have equal rights to work and have children at the same time. It would require recognition that women and men have biological differences and that the workplace cannot be structured solely around the biology of men, ignoring the biology of women. If this were the case, it would be impossible to consider the accommodation of pregnancy in the workplace as any kind of "preferential treatment" or discrimination against men. Rather, the failure to accommodate pregnancy would rightly be recognized as a form of discrimination against women that disadvantages them in the workplace and violates their right to sex equality.

# VIOLENCE AGAINST WOMEN

*The United States Supreme Court said that I had no constitutional right to police protection or enforcement of my restraining order. So if restraining orders are not enforced, then they're not worth the paper they're written on. . . . The emptiness I feel when I remember my daughters and the great life they might have lived—nothing can bring them back, nothing. What I can do, however, is to be a voice for the voiceless and women who are promised protection in America and then denied it in the moment they are in danger. . . . Our country has an obligation to stop domestic violence in its tracks.*[1]

—Jessica Lenahan (formerly Gonzales)

Rebecca, Leslie, and Katheryn Gonzales. (Jessica Lenahan)

Rebecca, Katheryn, and Leslie Gonzales were ten, eight, and seven years old when their father abducted them in violation of a restraining order and killed them. Their mother, Jessica Gonzales, had called the police repeatedly, begging them to enforce the restraining order, which they declined to do. Jessica Gonzales sued the police. Her case went to the Supreme Court, where it was dismissed because there was no basis for her lawsuit in the U.S. Constitution under the Due Process Clause of the Fourteenth Amendment.

*I can tell you this: rape is like having your soul torn out. . . . Women are raped because they are women.*[2]

—Christy Brzonkala

Christy Brzonkala, a freshman at Virginia Tech, sued the two varsity football players who raped her under the Violence Against Women Act of 1994. The private right of action in the law, which enabled her to bring this lawsuit, was struck down by the Supreme Court as unconstitutional. The court found there was no basis for it in the Commerce Clause of the Constitution, or the Equal Protection Clause of the Constitution.

Soon after the Fourteenth Amendment was adopted in 1868 following the Civil War, in a series of cases dealing with racial violence and discrimination, the Supreme Court established that the Equal Protection Clause of the Constitution prohibited only state action, not private action by individuals. Victims of gender-based violence have sought justice from the Constitution, basing their claims on the Equal Protection Clause, the Commerce Clause, and the Due Process Clause of the Fourteenth Amendment, all ultimately to no avail. **The ERA could provide a constitutional basis for claims of gender-based violence.**

Christy Brzonkala was a freshman at Virginia Polytechnic Institute in September 1994 when she met Antonio Morrison and James Crawford, both students on the varsity football team. Within thirty minutes of their meeting, according to Christy, the two men pinned her down on a bed in a dorm room and raped her repeatedly. After the rape, Morrison told Christy, "You better not have any fucking diseases," and later announced in the dining room, "I like to get girls drunk and fuck the shit out of them."[3] In early 1995, Christy filed a complaint against Morrison and Crawford with the university, under its Sexual Assault Policy. At the hearing Morrison admitted that he had had sexual contact with Christy even though she had said "no" twice. The university found him guilty of sexual assault and suspended him for two semesters. It found there was insufficient evidence to take action against Crawford.

In July of that year, Christy learned that Morrison was going to challenge his conviction under the Sexual Assault Policy and that another hearing would be required under the Abusive Conduct Policy, which had been in place before the Sexual Assault Policy. Even though the Sexual Assault Policy had been formally distributed before Christy was assaulted, it had not been published in the student handbook, a fact that Morrison used to challenge his conviction. After the second hearing, Morrison was again convicted and sentenced to suspension for two semesters, but instead of "sexual assault," his conduct was described as "using abusive language." Morrison again appealed his conviction and in August his punishment was set aside as "excessive" compared to other convictions under the Abusive Conduct Policy. The university did not inform Christy that Morrison's suspension had been lifted. When she learned from an article in the *Washington Post* that he would be back in school for the fall semester, on full athletic scholarship, Christy dropped out. A state grand jury did not find sufficient evidence to charge Morrison with rape, even though he had admitted to nonconsensual sex. For a time, Christy was suicidal.

In 1994, the same year Christy Brzonkala was raped on campus, Congress passed the Violence Against Women Act (VAWA) after concluding that bias in state criminal justice systems often deprived victims of gender-based violence of equal protection of the laws and that a uniform national approach to this problem was needed.[4] VAWA was intended to strengthen the investigation and prosecution of rape and other gender-based violence, provide restitution for victims, and create a legal avenue of recourse in federal court when state law enforcement failed to prosecute these crimes. Through this avenue of recourse, known legally as a private right of action, VAWA allowed anyone victimized by gender-based violence to seek compensation, punitive damages, and other appropriate relief from the federal courts to protect his or her "right to be free from crimes of violence motivated by gender."[5]

Championed by Senator Joe Biden, the Violence Against Women Act was opposed by Chief Justice William Rehnquist and others in the judiciary who felt that remedies for violence against women had no place in federal jurisdiction and who, in particular, expressed concern that allowing victims of gender-based violence to bring legal action would flood the courts with claims. In hearings on the bill, Senator Biden defended the private right of action. "For too long," he said, "we have ignored the fight of women to be free from the fear of attacks based on their gender."[6] Citing the fact that women were the target of 97 percent of all sexual assaults, he recognized violence against women as a civil rights violation. Many states had started to organize task forces to inquire into gender bias in the judiciary. Evidence of this clear bias— such as a probation officer questioning whether a nine-year-old was a "real victim," as he had heard she was a "tramp," or a judge commenting from the bench that a domestic violence victim "probably should have been hit"—was used to support the bill.[7] Following passage of the Violence Against Women Act, Senator Biden called it his "single most important legislative accomplishment."[8]

In December 1995, using the new federal law, Christy Brzonkala sued her two attackers, Morrison and Crawford, as well as Virginia Tech for its handling of her complaint against them. The district court in Virginia dismissed the case, finding that the private right of action under which Christy brought her case was unconstitutional because Congress lacked the authority to create a private right of action for victims of violence against women. Every other district court to consider this question had upheld the constitutionality of the VAWA right of action (in Rhode Island, Washington, New York, Illinois, Tennessee, Iowa, Connecticut, Nebraska, and Pennsylvania),[9] and the Fourth Circuit Court of Appeals initially reversed the district court's decision by a 2–1 vote of a three-judge panel.[10] However, the case was then reheard by the entire court of appeals, which reinstated the district court's decision to dismiss the case. Citing the "crude and derogatory" remarks made by Morrison as evidence of his "gender animus," the Fourth Circuit court recognized that Christy's claim fell within the scope of the new law. However, the court held that this part of the new law was unconstitutional because there was no basis of authority for it in the Constitution.[11]

Victims of gender-based violence have sought justice from the Constitution, basing their claims on the Equal Protection Clause, the Commerce Clause, and the Due Process Clause of the Fourteenth Amendment, all ultimately to no avail. The obvious place to look for authority in the Constitution to justify the right of a sexual assault victim to legal recourse would be the Equal Protection Clause. However, there is a long history of jurisprudence limiting the Fourteenth Amendment to state action and excluding action by private individuals from the scope of its protection.

As far back as 1883, the Supreme Court held that the Fourteenth Amendment did not give Congress the power to regulate private acts, striking down a number of civil rights laws passed soon after the Civil War to combat racial violence and discrimination in the wake of slavery. The Civil Rights Act of 1871 made it a crime for two or more persons to conspire to deprive anyone of equal protection of the laws. Sheriff R.G. Harris successfully challenged his indictment under this law after he led a lynch mob to a Tennessee jail, where they hauled out four black men and brutally beat them up, killing one of them. In *United States v. Harris*, the Supreme Court in 1883 struck down the Civil Rights Act of 1871, also known as the Ku Klux Klan Act, holding that it was unconstitutional for the federal government to criminalize private acts such as assault and murder because the Fourteenth Amendment regulated only state action.[12]

In five consolidated cases known as the *Civil Rights Cases*, the court struck down the Civil Rights Act of 1875, which prohibited discrimination in places of public accommodation, such as hotels and theaters.[13] The Supreme Court in these cases again held that the power of Congress to pass legislation to enforce the Fourteenth Amendment is a limited power, that the prohibition of discrimination is a prohibition only against state action, not a prohibition against discrimination by private individuals.[14]

Even in this first generation of Fourteenth Amendment jurisprudence in the nineteenth century, spirited debate took place over the meaning and scope of the Equal Protection Clause. It had been written in the context of ending slavery. The Citizenship Clause of the Fourteenth Amendment effectively overruled the Supreme Court's *Dred Scott* decision denying United States citizenship to the descendants of African slaves. In addition to protecting citizenship status for all Americans, the Fourteenth Amendment included the Due Process Clause and the Equal Protection Clause, which prohibit states from depriving anyone of life, liberty, or property without due process of law, or from denying anyone equal protection of the laws. Due process and equal protection are framed in the negative, as prohibitions on states rather than as affirmative obligations. While this construction lends itself to the limitation of state action imposed on it by the Supreme Court, it does not inevitably preclude the possibility of addressing private action, although it has been so interpreted.

The Civil Rights Acts of 1871 and 1875 were reviewed by the Supreme Court in the context of the Thirteenth Amendment as well as the Fourteenth Amendment. The Thirteenth Amendment, which prohibited slavery, clearly applies to private action—namely, the ownership of slaves. The court ruled, however, that the Thirteenth Amendment prohibited only slavery, not lynching or racial discrimination. Writing for the 8–1 majority in the *Civil Rights Cases* in 1883, Justice Joseph Bradley rejected the notion that denial of admission to places of public accommodation based on racial discrimination was a badge of slavery or any manner of servitude, writing:

It would be running the slavery argument into the ground to make it apply to every act of discrimination which a person may see fit to make as to guests he will entertain, or as to the people he will take into his coach or cab or car; or admit to his concert or theatre, or deal with in other matters of intercourse or business.[15]

In a Supreme Court decision ten years earlier, *Bradwell v. Illinois*, the same Justice Bradley had made his views on sex discrimination known, concurring that the Fourteenth Amendment did not entitle women admission to the bar. He explained, "The natural and proper timidity and delicacy which belongs to the female sex evidently unfits it for many of the occupations of civil life. . . . The paramount destiny and mission of woman are to fulfill the noble and benign offices of wife and mother. This is the law of the Creator."[16]

In the *Civil Rights Cases* on racial discrimination, Justice Bradley, having dismissed the Thirteenth Amendment as a constitutional basis for the Civil Rights Act of 1875, declined to answer the question of whether, with regard to the Fourteenth Amendment, a right to enjoy equal access to public accommodation was "one of the essential rights of the citizen which no State can abridge or interfere with." Under the Fourteenth Amendment, "conceding for the sake of argument" that it was such a protected right, Justice Bradley held that "the wrongful act of an individual, unsupported by [state] authority, is simply a private wrong," not an impairment of civil rights. He disparaged the law, which merely required equal treatment of African Americans in their access to places of public accommodation. "When a man has emerged from slavery," he said, "there must be some stage in the progress of his elevation when he takes the rank of a mere citizen and ceases to be the special favorite of the laws."[17]

In a compelling but lone dissent, Justice John Marshall Harlan took issue with this comment and suggested that it was "scarcely just to say that the colored race has been the special favorite of the laws."[18] He noted that "the one underlying purpose of Congressional legislation has been to enable the black race to take the rank of mere citizens" and that what Congress had hoped to accomplish with the Civil Rights Act of 1875 was "what had already been done in every State of the Union for the white race—to secure and protect rights belonging to them as freemen and citizens, nothing more."[19]

Justice Harlan defended the Civil Rights Act of 1875, highlighting the public functions of railroads, inns, and hotels and the impact of restricting access to them on the basis of race. He affirmed that this form of discrimination *was* a badge of servitude ensuing from slavery and explained the importance of including private action within the scope of the Fourteenth Amendment. "It was perfectly well known," he said, "that the great danger to the equal enjoyment by citizens of their rights as citizens was to be apprehended not altogether from unfriendly State legislation, but from the hostile actions of corporations and individuals in the States."[20] The intention of the amendment was to grant Congress the power to enforce the amendment through appropriate legislation, he said. He charged the majority with reading the language too narrowly. Rather than interpreting the prohibition of state action as a limitation on the power of Congress to enforce the amendment (i.e., by prohibiting only state action), he suggested that the prohibition of state action was intended simply to limit the power of states—to prohibit them from engaging in discriminatory action. Justice Harlan valiantly but unsuccessfully argued for an interpretation of the Equal Protection Clause that would enable Congress to address discrimination in private action as well as state action.

The outcome of the *Harris* case and the *Civil Rights Cases* had a long-term and severe impact on the ability of the Fourteenth Amendment to address discrimination effectively, with its reach limited to state action. Known as the Enforcement Act, the Civil Rights Act of 1875 was intended to enforce the Fourteenth Amendment promise that no person should be denied equal protection of the laws. However, in these early cases, the groundwork was laid for a narrow vision of the Fourteenth Amendment, and the idea that equal protection of the laws should be related to the realization of meaningful equality was rejected. The substantive goal of the Thirteenth and Fourteenth Amendments, taken together, was interpreted to be ending slavery, not ending discrimination and promoting equality.

In striking down the requirement in the Civil Rights Act of 1875 that all persons enjoy equal access to places of public accommodation, the Supreme Court noted that while private action was not subject to federal law under the Equal Protection Clause of the Fourteenth Amendment, it might be subject to federal law under the Commerce Clause. The court declined, however, to address this possibility. Article I of the Constitution gives Congress the power to regulate interstate commerce, and going forward it became a primary constitutional foundation for laws relating to discrimination. It was under this clause that the Civil Rights Act of 1964 was passed, and interstate commerce remains the central battleground for the assertion of federal jurisdiction over private acts of discrimination.

In passing the Violence Against Women Act in 1994, Congress relied as much, if not more, on the Commerce Clause as on the Fourteenth Amendment to provide a constitutional foundation for the legislation. The *Congressional Record* took note of the effect of gender-based violence on the national economy and interstate commerce, including increased health expenditure, reduced employment opportunity, and consumer spending.[21] Every year four million American women were battered by their husbands or partners, more than one million so severely that they sought medical help for resulting injuries.[22] Absenteeism from work due to domestic violence alone cost an estimated $3 billion to $5 billion every year, with an additional $5 billion to $10 billion spent every year on health care, criminal justice, and other costs related to domestic violence.[23]

In the first court cases brought under the Violence Against Women Act, the private right of action was upheld largely, if not exclusively, under the Commerce Clause. In striking down this provision of VAWA in Christy Brzonkala's case, the courts also focused largely on the Commerce Clause. The Fourth Circuit Court of Appeals recited the long-standing view that the Fourteenth Amendment was not intended to address private conduct, and suggested that to uphold the VAWA provision would extend its reach "beyond a point ever contemplated by the Supreme Court since that Amendment's ratification."[24] The Fourth Circuit court rejected the argument that violence against women was a widespread social problem that had an impact on the national economy and should therefore be within the constitutional authority of

Congress to address under the Commerce Clause of the Constitution. It also rejected the argument that gender bias in state criminal justice systems often denied women justice and that this denial by state actors violated the Equal Protection Clause of the Fourteenth Amendment.

The Commerce Clause of the Constitution has been broadly interpreted to uphold federal legislation on matters substantially affecting interstate commerce covering a wide range of activities. However, in a 5–4 decision, the Supreme Court affirmed the decision of the Fourth Circuit court that the VAWA private right of action was unconstitutional. The court's decision effectively dismissed the congressional finding that violence against women substantially affected interstate commerce. In a prior decision in 1995, the Supreme Court had struck down a federal law criminalizing possession of a gun within a thousand feet of any school on the grounds that this crime was "in no sense an economic activity that might, through repetition elsewhere, substantially affect any sort of interstate commerce." [25] Having drawn the line in this case by rejecting arguments that the costs of crime and its impact on national productivity bore a substantial relation to interstate commerce, the court held that "gender-motivated crimes of violence are not, in any sense of the phrase, economic activity." [26]

Violence against women was not an issue highlighted in the ERA campaign of the 1970s, and it is only more recently that it has come to be understood, in the United States and around the world, as a manifestation of sex discrimination and a violation of human rights. Both in law and practice, violence against women has been treated with greater lenience than other violent crimes. Historically, domestic violence and marital rape have not been recognized as criminal conduct, and even to this day distinctions in the law remain as vestiges of the deference given to men in the privacy of their homes, enabling them to perpetrate violence against women with impunity. Gender bias in the response of police, prosecutors, and judges has been increasingly highlighted as a form of state action, giving new life to claims made under the Fourteenth Amendment by victims of gender-based violence for equal protection of the laws.

In Christy Brzonkala's case, the Supreme Court acknowledged

the evidence underlying the congressional conclusion that pervasive bias in state courts results in "insufficient investigation and prosecution of gender-motivated crime, inappropriate focus on the behavior and credibility of the victims of that crime, and unacceptably lenient punishment for those who are actually convicted of gender-motivated violence."[27] However, the court reaffirmed that only state action is governed by the Fourteenth Amendment, citing the *Harris* and *Civil Rights Cases* of the 1880s, as well as *Shelley v. Kraemer*, a precedent from 1948 reaffirming that the Fourteenth Amendment "erects no shield against merely private conduct, however discriminatory or wrongful."[28] In that case, an African American family had purchased a house that had a racially restrictive covenant barring them from occupying it. While holding that the restrictive covenant was not itself invalid under the Fourteenth Amendment because it was an agreement between private parties, the Supreme Court held that enforcing the covenant through judicial action would constitute state action. Because there was no state action in Christy Brzonkala's case, the court held that it was not for the federal government to provide her with a remedy.

Writing for the majority in Christy Brzonkala's case, known as the *Morrison* case, Chief Justice William Rehnquist extensively discussed the nineteenth-century cases that struck down congressional efforts to address lynching and the exclusion of black men and women from public places. He rejected the argument that VAWA, unlike these precedents, was a response to gender-based discrimination by state authorities and therefore involved state action. The chief justice presented evidence that VAWA was like these earlier precedents and that they *too* had been addressing the biased implementation of the law. He recited excerpts from the legislative history of the civil rights legislation of the 1870s, which sound eerily familiar. Representative James Garfield had said in defense of the Civil Rights Act:

> [T]he chief complaint is not that the laws of the State are unequal, but that even where the laws are just and equal on their face, yet, by a systematic maladministration of them, or a

neglect or refusal to enforce their provisions, a portion of the people are denied equal protection under them.[29]

In addition to the length of time the old cases had been on the books, their doctrinal force was credited by the chief justice to the "insight attributable to the Members of the Court at that time" as they had all had "intimate knowledge and familiarity with the events surrounding the adoption of the Fourteenth Amendment."[30] Dismissing the view that these early cases had been wrongly decided, a view that had been expressed by Justice Tom Clark and Justice Brennan (and at the time Justice Harlan, with the same advantage of firsthand insight), Justice Rehnquist reaffirmed in the *Morrison* case the "enduring vitality of the *Civil Rights Cases* and *Harris*."[31]

Two dissenting opinions were filed in the *Morrison* case, only one of which—authored by Justice Stephen Breyer—even mentioned the Fourteenth Amendment. Like the majority of the court, the dissenting justices saw the case as being primarily about the Commerce Clause and the proper division of authority between the federal government and the states. In the context of the concern over federal encroachment of state power, Justice Breyer noted that thirty-eight state attorneys general, representing the "overwhelming majority" of states, had supported the Violence Against Women Act in a joint letter to Congress expressing their belief that "the problem of violence against women is a national one, requiring federal attention, federal leadership, and federal funds."[32] Justice Breyer mentioned the Fourteenth Amendment only at the end of his dissenting opinion, and he was joined in this brief section of his opinion by only one of the three justices who joined him in the Commerce Clause section of his opinion. He suggested that the failure of states to provide adequate remedies for gender-based violence, presumably thinking this might constitute state action, could provide a basis under the Equal Protection Clause for the constitutionality of the VAWA private right of action. However, he declined to address the question definitively, preferring to support VAWA as an exercise of congressional power under the Commerce Clause.

While the decision on the validity of VAWA was pending before the Supreme Court, Jessica Gonzales was, in 1999, in the midst of divorce proceedings in Castle Rock, Colorado. Because her husband, Simon, was a violent man, she obtained a court order of protection against him, requiring him to remain at least a hundred yards away from her and their three daughters. When one afternoon he came to the house and took the three girls, Jessica called the police for help. She showed the two officers who came to her home a copy of the court-issued restraining order, which had a printed notice to law enforcement directing them to make an arrest when there was reason to believe the order had been violated. The officers said there was nothing they could do and told Jessica to call the police department again in a few hours if the children had not returned by then.

An hour later Jessica learned that Simon Gonzales was with the children at an amusement park in Denver. She called the police again and asked them to go get her daughters, but the officer she spoke to said there was nothing they could do as Denver was outside their jurisdiction. She begged them to contact the Denver police, but they refused, instead telling her to wait a few hours and see if her husband brought the girls home. When she called the police back a few hours later to say her children were still missing, the police told her to wait until midnight. She called again at midnight and then went to the police station in person to beg the police to take action. She was met with indifference and told that the father of the children had a right to spend time with them. The police did not respond until Simon Gonzales showed up at the police station at 3 a.m. and opened fire on them, whereupon they returned fire and fatally shot him. The police subsequently found the three girls dead in the cab of his pickup truck. Rebecca, Katheryn, and Leslie Gonzales, ages ten, eight, and seven, had each been shot in the head.

Jessica sued the town of Castle Rock for the failure of its police to enforce the court's restraining order against her husband, claiming a violation of the Due Process Clause of the Fourteenth Amendment and alleging that the police department had "an official policy or custom of failing to respond properly to complaints of restraining order violations."[33] The Due Process Clause provides that no state shall "deprive any person of life, liberty, or property, without due process of law." The Supreme Court had already held, in a case decided in 1989, that the Due Process Clause does not "requir[e] the State to protect the life, liberty, and property of its citizens against invasion by private actors," but left open the possibility that once a state created certain rights to protection, they could not be taken away without due process.[34]

The district court dismissed the claim that Jessica Gonzales had an enforceable right to protection under the restraining order she had gotten from the court. However, on appeal, the Tenth Circuit court partially reversed this decision, on the theory that Jessica Gonzales had a "protected property interest" in the enforcement of the restraining order, of which she could not be deprived without due process.[35] While rejecting, in accordance with Supreme Court precedent, the argument that Jessica and her daughters had an inherent constitutional right to police protection from her husband, the appeals court found that once the state court issued the restraining order with mandatory enforcement provisions, Jessica Gonzales was entitled to its enforcement. By repeatedly ignoring and refusing her requests for enforcement, the police had deprived her of this entitlement. Because of her claim that this deprivation resulted from the custom and policy of the police department not to enforce domestic violence orders of protection, rather than from random and unauthorized acts, the court held that there were grounds for a finding of liability against the town of Castle Rock.

The town of Castle Rock appealed this decision, and in 2004 it was reversed by the Supreme Court. Despite the language taken directly from the law itself and printed on the restraining order mandating the police to enforce it, the Supreme Court held that "[w]e do not believe that these provisions of Colorado law truly made enforcement of restraining orders mandatory. A well-established tradition of police discretion has long coexisted with apparently mandatory arrest statutes."[36] Despite statutes that "seem to preclude non-enforcement by the police," the court suggested that "such statutes cannot be interpreted literally." In other words, although the law mandated arrest for violation of the court order, arrest was not mandatory.[37]

Writing for the majority, Justice Scalia scorned the Tenth Circuit Court of Appeals for suggesting that the lack of a right to enforcement "would render domestic abuse restraining orders utterly valueless."[38] Justice Scalia suggested that the existence of a restraining order for

Simon Gonzales—the establishment of a legal framework for arrest and criminal prosecution—was "hardly 'valueless,' even if the prospect of those sanctions ultimately failed to prevent him from committing three murders and a suicide."[39] What value the restraining order had to Jessica Gonzales is not at all clear, in light of this outcome.

Narrowly focusing on the challenges of a mandate to make an arrest in cases where the offender is not on-site, and on what he considered to be the "indeterminacy" of the mandate, Justice Scalia failed to consider the circumstances of the case in front of the Court—that the whereabouts of the offender were known and reported to the police and that despite repeated requests from Jessica Gonzales, the police demonstrated utter indifference to the obligation they had to undertake any enforcement action whatsoever when the violation of the order was reported. In any event, Justice Scalia said even if the enforcement of the restraining order could be said to be mandatory, "that would not necessarily mean that state law gave *respondent* [Jessica Gonzales] an entitlement to *enforcement* of the mandate," suggesting hers was an incidental or indirect benefit.[40] Finally, Justice Scalia suggested that even if there were an entitlement to enforcement of a restraining order, such an entitlement could in no way constitute a "property interest" of the sort protected by the Due Process Clause of the Constitution. The justice noted that the right to enforcement of a restraining order has no monetary value and that it "would not, of course, resemble any traditional conception of property."[41] His conclusion was that Jessica Gonzales "did not, for purposes of the Due Process Clause, have a property interest in police enforcement of the restraining order against her husband" and more generally that "the benefit that a third party may receive from having someone else arrested for a crime generally does not trigger protections under the Due Process Clause."[42]

In a dissenting opinion, Justice John Paul Stevens suggested that the court was giving "short shrift" to the uniqueness of mandatory arrest statutes in the context of domestic violence. He characterized the elimination of police discretion in this area as the "unmistakable goal" of these statutes, which were passed across the country specifically to address what he characterized as the "crisis of police under-enforcement" in the context of domestic violence. The perception by police that domestic violence was "a private, 'family' matter and that arrest was to be used as a last resort" was a cause of this crisis, according to Justice Stevens.[43] Mandatory arrest was the legislative response, designed to be truly mandatory precisely to remove the discretion that enabled this perception to limit effective police response to domestic violence. In this case, that discretion had resulted in the deaths of Rebecca, Katheryn, and Leslie Gonzales.

Dismissing Justice Scalia's concern about the "indeterminacy" of the enforcement mandate, Justice Stevens reviewed the language of the law specifically requiring the police to make an arrest or to issue an arrest warrant. While dependent on the circumstances, the mandate was for police to enforce the order, and, as he put it, "they lacked the discretion to do nothing." Because there is no discretion, Justice Stevens opined, "the new mandatory statutes undeniably create an entitlement to police enforcement of restraining orders."[44]

In considering the property rights protected by the Due Process Clause of the Constitution, Justice Stevens said it was "simply wrong to assert that a citizen's interest in the government's commitment to provide police enforcement in certain defined circumstances does not resemble any 'traditional conception of property.'"[45] He listed the numerous forms of intangible property that had been recognized by the court as property interests, such as public education. He noted that if Jessica Gonzales had hired a security firm to protect herself and her three daughters, her contract with that firm would have given rise to a property interest protected by the Due Process Clause of the Constitution. He likened the Colorado law and the judicial order of protection issued under the law to such a contract, creating a right that would similarly qualify for constitutional protection, and he concluded that the failure of the police to respond properly to reports of restraining order violations would clearly constitute a due process violation. His view, however, was shared by only one other Supreme Court colleague, Justice Ruth Bader Ginsburg.

Following the decision of the Supreme Court in the *Morrison* case, holding that neither the Commerce Clause of the Constitution nor the Equal Protection Clause of the Fourteenth Amendment gave Christy Brzonkala a right to challenge the impunity enjoyed by her rapist, in the *Castle Rock* case, the Supreme Court ruled out the Due Process Clause of the Fourteenth Amendment as an avenue of recourse for Jessica Gonzales. In this case, inexcusable police inaction led to the death of her three young daughters, whose murder by their father might well have been prevented had the police responded to her call telling them where he was and begging them to go and arrest him. The police were legally bound to do so by the restraining order against Simon Gonzales, which his wife had gotten from a court specifically to protect her from exactly these circumstances. Despite the Fourteenth Amendment's promise of equal protection under the laws, the Supreme Court denied justice to Christy Brzonkala, Jessica Gonzales, and all of the women who find themselves in similar circumstances.

Having exhausted all avenues of recourse in the United States when the Supreme Court decided *Castle Rock,* Jessica Gonzales (now Lenahan) brought her case to the Inter-American Commission on Human Rights. The Inter-American Commission is a regional human rights body for the Americas that was established in 1959 by the Organization of American States, which includes the United States among its members. In 2011, the Inter-American Commission found that the failure of the United States to act with due diligence to protect Jessica and her daughters from domestic violence was a violation of its obligations under the American Declaration of Human Rights not to discriminate on the basis of sex.[46] Article II of the American Declaration provides that "[a]ll persons are equal before the law . . . without distinction as to race, sex, language, creed or any other factor."

In its decision, the commission recalled that in practice, its equality provision means that nation-states, including the United States, "have the obligation to adopt the measures necessary to recognize and guarantee the effective equality of all persons before the law." The commission recognized gender-based violence as "one of the most extreme and pervasive forms of discrimination" and held that "a State's failure to act with due diligence to protect women from violence constitutes a form of discrimination, and denies women their right to equality before the law." The commission further noted that a state can be held responsible for the conduct of nonstate actors in certain circumstances, including its failure to prevent, prosecute, and sanction acts of domestic violence perpetrated by private individuals."[47] The commission called on the United States government to investigate and address systemic failures in law enforcement and made several recommendations to this end.

The United Nations special rapporteur on violence against women visited the United States in 2011. In her report on the visit, she highlighted a number of efforts that had been undertaken to address violence against women but also observed "a lack of legally binding federal provisions providing substantive protection against or prevention of acts of violence against women," resulting in "the continued prevalence of violence against women and discriminatory treatment of its victims, with a particularly detrimental impact on poor, minority and immigrant women."[48] She mentioned the Violence Against Women Act, noting that its intentions were laudable, but expressed concern over the Supreme Court jurisprudence, citing *Morrison* and *Castle Rock*. "The effect of these cases," the special rapporteur said, "is that even where local and state police are grossly negligent in their duties to protect women's right to physical security, and even where they fail to respond to an urgent call, there is no federal level constitutional or statutory remedy."

In the early days of the Fourteenth Amendment, Justice Harlan had foreseen the need for legislation "of a primary direct character," such as the Civil Rights Act of 1875, to implement the new constitutional right to be free from discrimination. Congress had the right, he contended, to "enforce and protect any right derived from or created by the national Constitution." He criticized the majority decision as "too narrow and artificial," and he wisely suggested, "It is not the words of the law, but the internal sense of it that makes the law; the letter of the law is the body; the sense and reason of the law is the soul."[49]

At a press conference a few days before the oral argument in her VAWA case at the Supreme Court, Christy Brzonkala declined to recount the details of her rape. "I don't want to keep reliving it," she said. "But I can tell you this: rape is like having your soul torn out." Christy told the press, "Women are raped because they are women."[50] Although by 2005 all states and the U.S. military finally eliminated the exemption from penalty for rape in marriage, twenty-six states still have lesser protection for victims, including lesser penalties and shorter reporting periods for sexual and violent crimes that occur in marriage. Denying women effective protection of the law in cases of rape and domestic violence, because these crimes are not taken as seriously as other violent crimes, is a form of discrimination against women. The Supreme Court has said clearly and repeatedly that this form of discrimination is without constitutional remedy.

As the jurisprudence demonstrates, victims of gender-based violence have made every effort to find effective recourse within the existing legal framework. Their quest for justice has been denied under the Equal Protection Clause of the Fourteenth Amendment on the grounds that only state action is covered. It has been denied under the Commerce Clause on the grounds that violence against women is unrelated to interstate commerce. It has been denied under the Due Process Clause of the Fourteen Amendment on the grounds that police protection is not a "property interest" worthy of due process rights. Violence against women is widely recognized as a form of sex discrimination. The Equal Rights Amendment would provide a proper constitutional foundation for effective action to end this discrimination, which deprives women of their most fundamental right to life.

# DISCRIMINATORY LAWS

"Every constitution written since the end of World War II includes a provision that men and women are citizens of equal stature. Ours does not. I have three granddaughters. I'd like them to be able to take out their Constitution and say, 'Here is a basic premise of our system, that men and women are persons of equal stature.' But it's not in there. We just have the equal protection clause, which everyone knows was not meant in the 1860s to change anything with regard to women's status. Women didn't get to vote until 1920."[1] —Supreme Court Justice Ruth Bader Ginsburg (Steve Petteway, courtesy of Collection of the Supreme Court of the United States)

With financial backing from the Laundry Owners' Association, Curt Muller, who owned a laundry business in Portland at the turn of the twentieth century, appealed his conviction for hiring Emma Gotcher, a female employee, to work more than ten hours in one day. He argued that the law limiting women's work to ten hours a day interfered with their contract rights. In 1908, the Supreme Court upheld the law, noting that "as healthy mothers are essential to vigorous offspring, the physical well-being of woman becomes an object of public interest and care in order to preserve the strength and vigor of the race." [2] Historically, discriminatory laws that were passed to protect women were considered beneficial to women.

Men marched for the right to drink beer in Oklahoma, where the sale of 3.2-percent beer to males under twenty-one was prohibited, while females over eighteen were allowed to buy this beer. Curtis Craig, an eighteen-year-old man, together with a licensed vendor of 3.2-percent beer, challenged the law in court, leading to a landmark Supreme Court case in 1976, *Craig v. Boren*, which heightened the level of review to "intermediate scrutiny" for sex discrimination cases. [3]

In many of its decisions, the Supreme Court has focused on equal *treatment* under the Fourteenth Amendment, rather than actual equality between men and women. An equal treatment approach, which is gender neutral, does not factor in the history of discrimination against women. In mandating equal treatment of men and women who are similarly situated, this approach does not effectively address the fact that men and women are generally *not* similarly situated. The entrenched historical inequality between the sexes cannot be erased by the creation of a level playing field because the players themselves are at two different levels. For the vast majority of women who have substantially less to begin with than men, a level playing field will only serve to keep them at the same lower level. **An ERA intended to promote sex equality could help ensure that equal means *really* equal.**

Over the past few decades, in large part because of the public awareness raised by the women's movement of the blatant legal inequalities between women and men, quite a number of laws explicitly discriminating on the basis of sex have been rescinded or amended. Nevertheless, some such laws remain, and there is an extensive body of jurisprudence on the distinctions based on sex and other classifications that are permissible under the Equal Protection Clause of the Fourteenth Amendment. One such law, upheld by the Supreme Court in 2001, relates to citizenship. Children who are born overseas to unwed parents, one of whom is an American citizen, have different rights to United States citizenship depending on whether they have an American mother or an American father. This law, based on gender stereotypes, explicitly discriminates against American fathers and their children. Even if paternity is acknowledged and documented, and even if an American father desperately wants to transmit citizenship to his son or daughter, the Immigration and Nationality Act governing citizenship for children born out of wedlock imposes additional requirements on American fathers not applicable to American mothers in the same situation.[4] While children born overseas to American mothers are held to have acquired U.S. citizenship at birth, an American father must take certain legal steps to register a relationship with his child born overseas before that child reaches the age of majority. Otherwise, that child loses the right to claim U.S. citizenship.

Tuan Anh Nguyen was born in 1969 in Vietnam to unwed parents—an American father and a Vietnamese mother. At the age of six, Tuan Anh came as a refugee to the United States, where he was raised in Texas by his father, Joseph Boulais. Joseph never legally adopted his son. Tuan Anh was a lawful permanent resident, but he never applied for naturalized citizenship. In 1992, at the age of twenty-two, Tuan Anh pled guilty to charges of criminal conduct and was sentenced to eight years imprisonment. His conviction for felony offenses led the Immigration and Naturalization Service to initiate deportation proceedings against him. Joseph went to court and obtained an order of parentage for Tuan Anh while the deportation appeal was pending, but the appeal was dismissed because Joseph had not complied with the requirement of the law that he officially register his paternal relationship with his son before Tuan Anh reached the age of majority. It was too late, and the Board of Immigration Appeals upheld the order of deportation.

Tuan Anh and his father together appealed to the courts for relief from his deportation. The Fifth Circuit court rejected their claim that the law violates the right to equal protection by setting forth different citizenship rules for children born overseas to unwed parents, depending on the sex of the citizen parent. The Supreme Court, by a 5–4 majority, affirmed the decision and upheld the constitutionality of the law, asserting that the difference in the requirements imposed by Congress on unmarried fathers and mothers was based on the "significant difference between their respective relationships to the potential citizen at the time of birth."[5] The court articulated two governmental interests underlying these requirements: the first was the importance of assuring paternity, and the second was the interest in ensuring that the child and parent have an opportunity to "develop a relationship that consists of real, everyday ties providing a connection between child and citizen parent."[6] Because of the mother's presence at birth, the court found that she inherently has this opportunity but that it is not inevitable in the case of a father, who may not even know that his child has been conceived. Requiring a father to demonstrate this relationship sometime in the first eighteen years of his child's life, the court held, was a means "in substantial furtherance of an important governmental objective," and it found the fit between the means and the end to be "exceedingly persuasive."[7]

The real reason for passage of this law was that, with so many American servicemen overseas, the government wanted to prevent children born as a result of their R&R activities abroad from claiming American citizenship. This reason was openly acknowledged by Justice Anthony Kennedy, who wrote the majority opinion for the court:

One concern in this context has always been with young men on duty with the Armed Forces in foreign countries. Today, the ease of travel and willingness of Americans to visit foreign countries have resulted in numbers of trips abroad that must be of real concern when contemplating the prospect of mandating, contrary to Congress' wishes, citizenship by male parentage subject to no condition other than the father's residence in this country. Equal protection principles do not require Congress to ignore this reality.[8]

In effect, the citizenship law was designed to accommodate irresponsible men who fathered children overseas, often while serving in the military, and abandoned these children after returning to the United States. Justice Kennedy cited statistics for 1969, the year in which Tuan Anh Nguyen was born, noting that there were 3,458,072 military personnel on duty in foreign countries, only 39,506 of whom were female.[9] He noted that the passage of time had only strengthened the argument for restricting citizenship as "the ease of travel and the willingness of Americans to visit foreign countries have resulted in numbers of trips abroad. . . . In 1999 alone, Americans made almost 25 million trips abroad, excluding trips to Canada and Mexico." Justice Kennedy also pointed out that "especially in light of the number of Americans who take short sojourns abroad, the prospect that a father might not even know of the conception is a realistic possibility."[10] Recognizing that paternity can be established by DNA, Justice Kennedy suggested that the importance of this interest was "too profound to be satisfied merely by conducting a DNA test."[11] Such a test did not ensure contact between father and child during the child's minority, a contact not required between mother and child beyond the moment of birth.

Protecting the American men who travel around the world sowing their seed without regard to consequence, the Supreme Court upheld this discriminatory law, which deprived a responsible parent, Joseph Boulais, of the son he had raised and lived with for sixteen years. Rather than serving his term of imprisonment in the United States, Tuan Anh Nguyen was subject to deportation from the only country he knew as his home and the life he had had with his father from the age of six, when in fact he would have been a U.S. citizen from birth if his mother rather than his father had been the American citizen, even if she had abandoned him immediately thereafter.

The four justices who dissented from this decision included the two women serving on the Supreme Court at the time, Justice Sandra Day O'Connor and Justice Ruth Bader Ginsburg. Written by Justice O'Connor, the dissent noted that the citizenship law treated mothers and fathers who were both present at the birth of their child differently solely on the basis of sex. "This type of treatment," Justice O'Connor said, "is patently inconsistent with the promise of equal protection of the laws." [12]

Justice O'Connor suggested that the law was supported by gender stereotypes of parental roles, not biological differences. The assumption in the discriminatory citizenship law is that mothers are more likely than fathers to develop meaningful relationships with their children, and the message, endorsed by the Supreme Court, is that fatherhood is optional even when established by DNA. As Justice O'Connor's dissent noted, the law is "paradigmatic of a historic regime that left women with responsibility, and freed men from responsibility, for non-marital children." [13] The conduct of American servicemen overseas and the opportunities they had "to interact with citizens of foreign countries" bore little relation, she said, to the question of whether the discriminatory law was a permissible governmental response to the circumstances. "Indeed," Justice O'Connor suggested, "the majority's discussion may itself simply reflect the stereotype of male irresponsibility that is no more a basis for the validity of the classification than are stereotypes about the 'traditional' behavior patterns of women." [14] Joseph Boulais was exceptional. Many young children, growing up with blue eyes or curly hair in Vietnam, were abandoned by their mothers as well as their fathers and ostracized by the community. They dreamed of finding their fathers in America. But in a 1970 statement, the U.S. Defense Department said, "The care and welfare of these unfortunate children . . . has never been and is not now considered an area of government responsibility." [15] The citizenship law went even further by legitimizing the failure of fathers to take responsibility for their Amerasian children, with a seal of approval from the Supreme Court.

In reviewing the law in the *Nguyen* case, the court applied a test known as "intermediate scrutiny." Through its jurisprudence on cases of discrimination brought under the Equal Protection Clause of the Fourteenth Amendment, the Supreme Court has established a hierarchy of tests for laws that are explicitly discriminatory. Under the lowest level of scrutiny, known as the rational basis test, a law is constitutional if its purpose is *rationally related* to a *legitimate* government interest. Under intermediate scrutiny, a law must be *substantially related* to an *important* government interest to be upheld as constitutional. Under the most rigorous test, strict scrutiny, a law must be *necessary* to achieve a *compelling* government interest, or else it will be struck down as unconstitutional. In summary, the courts make a judgment about the constitutionality of a law by looking to its means and its purpose, subjecting it to a given level of scrutiny (rational basis, intermediate scrutiny, or strict scrutiny).

It is clear that in varying circumstances, a law might pass one, or two, but not all three of these tests. The *Nguyen* case is one such example. It was reviewed using the standard of "intermediate scrutiny," requiring that there be an "important government purpose" of the law and that the law be "substantially related" to that purpose. The purpose of the citizenship law as articulated by the Supreme Court was twofold: the importance of assuring paternity and an interest in ensuring an opportunity for the child and parent to have a meaningful relationship. This purpose was reasonably deemed "important" and might well have even been deemed "compelling" under a higher standard of review. The requirements set forth in the law certainly relate to this purpose. The question for the court was whether the requirements were *substantially* related to the purpose of ensuring that there is an opportunity for a meaningful relationship between parents and children born outside marriage. As the dissent pointed out, many other sex-neutral alternatives could have been adopted, such as the presence of the parent at birth. If the real interest was to ensure that a relationship actually developed between child and parent, then that might also have been established in a sex-neutral way and the requirement could have applied to mothers as well as fathers. The court divided 5–4 on whether the citizenship law requirements for men only were a means "substantially related" to the government's purpose.

To uphold the citizenship law in the *Nguyen* case under a standard of "strict scrutiny," the Supreme Court would have had to find that its requirements were "necessary" to achieve the intended purpose. The availability of sex-neutral alternatives to achieve this purpose, some even mentioned by the majority in its opinion, would render the sex-based discriminatory requirements of the law unnecessary and therefore impermissible under this higher standard of review. However, under "intermediate scrutiny," the fact that comparable sex-neutral alternatives could be used to achieve the same purpose does not preclude a finding that the sex-discriminatory requirements are "substantially related" to the achievement of the government's purpose and therefore permissible.

The differing levels of review, as demonstrated by the *Nguyen* case, mean that the protection from discrimination offered by the Equal Protection Clause is not equal for all classes of people. "Suspect" classifications such as race and religion are judged by the highest standard of "strict scrutiny," while sex has been granted an "intermediate" standard of review as a "quasi-suspect" classification. If the *Nguyen* case had been judged by the stricter standard of scrutiny to which racial or religious discrimination is subjected, the Supreme Court would almost certainly have required the same treatment of U.S. citizen fathers and U.S. citizen mothers with regard to the transmission of citizenship to their children.

When for the first time, in 1971, the Supreme Court reviewed a sex discriminatory law under the Fourteenth Amendment using this equal protection analysis, it applied the traditional "rational basis" test. In this case, Richard Reed, a minor in Idaho, had died without a will. His parents, Sally and Cecil Reed, separated at the time of Richard's death, both filed petitions in the probate court, each seeking to be named the administrator of their deceased son's estate. The law provided that if there was more than one person equally entitled to administer the state, "males must be preferred to females." For this reason, the probate court appointed Cecil Reed as administrator. Sally challenged the law, arguing that the Fourteenth Amendment prohibited discrimination on the basis of sex. The Supreme Court agreed, concluding that "the arbitrary preference established in favor of males by §15-314 of the Idaho Code cannot stand in the face of the Fourteenth Amendment's command that no State deny the equal protection of the laws to any person within its jurisdiction." [16] The court found that differentiating on the basis of sex in granting letters of estate administration bore no rational relationship to a government interest. It invalidated the law as unconstitutional in 1971.

The "intermediate" standard of review applied in the *Nguyen* case was first developed in a 1973 case relating to benefits in the armed services. The challenged law allowed men to claim their wives as "dependents" regardless of whether they were actually dependent on their husbands, while women in the armed services could claim their husbands as "dependents" only if they were in fact dependent on their wives. Sharron Frontiero, a lieutenant in the air force, challenged the denial of "dependent" status to her husband, Joseph, claiming that the sex discrimination in the benefits offered by the armed services to men and women in its ranks was a violation of the Constitution. In this case, *Frontiero v. Richardson*, the Supreme Court held that departure from the traditional "rational basis" analysis for review of classifications based on sex was "clearly justified" and recalled the "long and unfortunate history of sex discrimination" in the country. Sex was differentiated from other classifications and considered "suspect" because, according to the court, "the sex characteristic frequently bears no relation to ability to perform or contribute to society." Consequently, "statutory distinctions between the sexes often have the effect of invidiously relegating the entire class of females to inferior legal status without regard to the actual capabilities of its individual members." Considering also the recent initiatives by Congress to address sex discrimination, including the Equal Pay Act and Title VII of the Civil Rights Act, and the passage by Congress of the Equal Rights Amendment in 1972, the court concluded that sex-based classifications, like race-based classifications, are "inherently suspect, and must therefore be subjected to strict judicial scrutiny." [17]

The plurality opinion in *Frontiero* was written by Justice William Brennan, joined by Justice William Douglas, Justice Byron White, and Justice Thurgood Marshall. Justice Lewis Powell wrote a concurring opinion, joined by Chief Justice Warren Burger and Justice Harry Blackmun. While agreeing that the law was unconstitutional, Justice Powell disagreed with the view that all sex-based classifications should be inherently suspect and subject to strict scrutiny. For the purpose of the case at hand, he felt that even under the traditional "rational relationship" test of constitutionality, the law could not be upheld in any event. The Equal Rights Amendment had been passed by Congress and submitted to the states for ratification, and until it was adopted, he felt it would be premature to add "sex" to the list of inherently suspect classifications.[18]

In 1976, the Supreme Court reviewed a law from Oklahoma prohibiting the sale of 3.2-percent beer to males under the age of twenty-one and females under the age of eighteen. The law was challenged by Curtis Craig, an eighteen-year-old man, together with Carolyn Whitener, a licensed vendor of 3.2-percent beer. Previously in Oklahoma, the age of majority had been eighteen for women and twenty-one for men, and the age of adult criminal responsibility had been eighteen for women and sixteen for men. These age differentials were struck down as unconstitutional by the Tenth Circuit Court of Appeals in 1972, and the age of majority for both men and women was set at eighteen. With regard to the sale of beer, however, the court noted, "public health and safety represents an important function of state and local governments."[19] Statistics submitted to the court indicated that in Oklahoma, young men aged eighteen to twenty were arrested for drunkenness ten times as often as young women of the same age, and for drunk driving almost eighteen times as often. Nationwide, during a five-year period from 1967 to 1972, arrests of those under eighteen for drunken driving increased 138 percent, with 93 percent of all those arrested being young men.[20]

The district court upheld the Oklahoma law, finding on the basis of this evidence that there was a rational basis for the legislation under challenge—namely, the interest of the state in enhancement of traffic safety. The Supreme Court disagreed, looking at the Oklahoma statistics that indicated while 0.18 percent of young women were arrested for drunk driving, 2 percent of young men (more than ten times the number of young women) were arrested for drunk driving. The court felt that while this disparity was "not trivial in a statistical sense," it could not be used to justify a gender-based distinction in the law.[21] As Justice Stevens put it in his concurring opinion, "The legislation imposes a restraint on 100% of the males in the class allegedly because about 2% of them have probably violated one or more laws relating to the consumption of alcoholic beverages. . . . [I]t does not seem to me that an insult to all of the young men of the State can be justified by visiting the sins of the 2% on the 98%."[22] The court cited its *Reed* decision, but it found that "the relationship between gender and traffic safety becomes far too tenuous to satisfy *Reed*'s requirement that the gender-based difference be substantially related to achievement of the statutory objective."[23] The court struck down the law as "a denial of equal protection of the laws to males aged 18–20."[24]

In his concurring opinion, Justice Powell agreed with the outcome but expressed reservations with regard to the appropriate standard for equal protection analysis. He said, "The Court has had difficulty in agreeing upon a standard of equal protection analysis that can be applied consistently to the wide variety of legislative classifications. There are valid reasons for dissatisfaction with the 'two tier' approach." He recognized that "our decision today will be viewed by some as a 'middle tier' approach. While I would not endorse that characterization and would not welcome a further subdividing of equal protection analysis, candor compels the recognition that the relatively deferential 'rational basis' standard of review normally applied takes on a sharper focus when we address a gender-based classification."[25] Justice Stevens, also concurring, expressed concern over "what has become known as the two-tiered analysis of equal protection claims" and suggested that really it was a "method the Court has employed to explain decisions that actually apply a single standard in a reasonably consistent fashion."[26] He noted that "[m]en as a general class have not been the victims of the kind of historic, pervasive discrimination that has disadvantaged other groups."[27]

Chief Justice Burger dissented, and said of the standard of review used by the court, "Though today's decision does not go so far as to make gender-based classifications 'suspect,' it makes gender a disfavored classification." The means employed by the Oklahoma legislature were clearly rational, even if others found them to be "unwise, unneeded, or possibly even a bit foolish."[28] In another dissent, Justice Rehnquist also criticized the court's enunciation of a new standard. He scorned the language of intermediate review, that a law treating men less favorably than women "must serve important governmental objectives and must be substantially related to achievement of those objectives" as coming "out of thin air."[29] Justice Rehnquist warned the court, "We have had enough difficulty with the two standards of review which our cases have recognized—the norm of 'rational basis,' and the 'compelling state interest' required where a 'suspect classification' is involved—so as to counsel weightily against the insertion of still another 'standard' between those two."[30]

Justice Rehnquist also pointed out, as "the only redeeming feature of the Court's opinion," that it signaled a retreat from the views expressed by the plurality opinion in *Frontiero* that sex was a "suspect" classification subject to strict scrutiny for purposes of equal protection analysis. He recalled that in *Frontiero*, the reasons put forward for this classification centered on the "long and unfortunate history of sex discrimination" in the United States.[31] The range of legal restrictions on women, including ownership of property and participation in the electoral process, had the effect, the *Frontiero* decision had said, of "relegating the entire class of females to inferior legal status without regard to the actual capabilities of its individual members." Justice Rehnquist asked why the Oklahoma statute should be subject to "an elevated or 'intermediate' level of scrutiny, like that invoked in cases dealing with discrimination against females." Without the history of past discrimination such as that relied on in the *Frontiero* decision for its invocation of strict scrutiny, to his mind there was no justification for a higher level of scrutiny in this case involving discrimination against men than in cases of discrimination against women. "There is no suggestion in the Court's opinion," he observed, "that males in this age group are in any way peculiarly disadvantaged, subject to systematic discriminatory treatment, or otherwise in need of special solicitude from the courts."[32]

For this reason, Justice Rehnquist believed the Oklahoma law should be reviewed under the traditional "rational basis" test, rather than a heightened standard of scrutiny. His analysis of the statistics on drunk driving was not focused on the numbers themselves but on their relationship to each other. The question was not whether 2 percent of men arrested was high or low, but how much higher it was than the 0.18 percent of women arrested, "whether the incidence of drunk driving among young men is sufficiently greater than among young women to justify differential treatment." Justice Rehnquist considered the evidence to suggest "clear differences between the drinking and driving habits of young men and women," and that these differences were enough for the state to reasonably conclude that young men posed a far greater hazard to highway safety. "[T]he gender-based difference in treatment in this case is therefore not irrational," he said.[33]

Justice Rehnquist recognized in his dissent that men are differently situated than women. Traditionally, women have been victimized by sex discrimination, while men have more often been its perpetrators. But the underlying principle of providing additional benefit or protection for those who have been historically subject to discrimination is only one of several themes running through the jurisprudence. Another theme is the right to equal treatment, which is blind to the differences between the sexes, including their relative treatment historically. It is ironic that the heightened standard of scrutiny for sex-based discrimination comes from a case about men's right to buy beer, brought not only by a young man adversely affected by the law but also by a vendor whose interest was in selling beer. This scenario is very different from the one in which women are given secondary rights to men in the appointment of estate administrators, or in which women's rights to employment benefits for their husbands are narrower than men's rights to employment benefits for their wives, based on stereotypes of dependency that assume wives are dependent on their husbands, and husbands are not dependent on their wives.

Equal treatment in many of the cases is the issue that has been adjudicated by the Supreme Court rather than the more fundamental notion of actual equality between men and women, which recognizes that women have been historically disadvantaged. An equal treatment approach inherently leads to gender neutrality, where the issue is not discrimination against women but equal treatment of men and women who are similarly situated. This approach tends to preserve the status quo. It has not effectively addressed the fact that men and women are generally *not* similarly situated. Men, as well as women, have benefited from the Fourteenth Amendment's guarantee of equal protection in some cases, but the jurisprudence has evolved in such a way that it is largely blind to the inequality between the sexes and the history of discrimination against women, even though that history is what led to the recognition of the need for heightened scrutiny of laws with distinctions based on sex.

The exclusion of women from educational settings is another form of explicit discrimination that the Fourteenth Amendment has addressed within the framework of equal treatment for men and women who are equally qualified. In 1996, the Supreme Court held that the Virginia Military Institute (VMI), a single-sex school for men that received state funding, was required to admit women who met the same qualifications as men. The Fourth Circuit court had initially ordered VMI to remedy the constitutional violation and had accepted as a remedy the creation of a parallel program for women, the Virginia Women's Institute for Leadership at a private liberal arts women's college, finding the new program to be "substantively comparable" to VMI.[34] But the Supreme Court disagreed and struck down VMI's male-only admissions policy.[35] At around the same time, in 1993, Shannon Faulkner applied to The Citadel in South Carolina, the country's only other state-supported all-male military college. A student with a 4.0 grade point average, Shannon deleted all references to her sex on the application and was accepted for admission. When The Citadel learned she was female, it rescinded its offer to her. The district court ordered her admission, and the Fourth Circuit court affirmed the order.[36] In 1995, Shannon enrolled, the only woman in the class, entering the school with an escort of United States marshals. She had received a number of threats, including one that her parents would be killed.[37] Five days later, Shannon dropped out, citing emotional and psychological abuse. At the time, the male cadets openly celebrated her departure. However, since then, hundreds of women have graduated from The Citadel.

In 1972, Title IX was added to the Education Amendments Act, prohibiting any educational program or activity that receives federal financial assistance from discriminating on the basis of sex. Title IX was patterned after Title VI of the Civil Rights Act of 1964, which prohibits entities that receive federal financial assistance from discriminating on the basis of race, color, or national origin. Later, both the Age Discrimination Act and Section 504 of the Rehabilitation Act of 1973 adopted similar prohibitions for entities receiving federal financial assistance, for discrimination based on age and disability, respectively.

Title IX has had a dramatic impact in promoting educational equality for girls and women. For a decade after its passage, courts uniformly ruled that a recipient of federal financial assistance could not discriminate in any aspect of its program. But in 1984, the Supreme Court took a different approach. In *Grove City v. Bell*, the court affirmed that Grove City College, a private coeducational school in Pennsylvania, was subject to Title IX because it admitted students who benefited from federally funded scholarships. However, the court declined to apply Title IX to Grove City College as a whole, instead limiting its application only to the financial aid program of the college that actually received the federal financial assistance.[38] This decision left all the Grove City College programs and activities *other* than financial aid free from the prohibition against discrimination on the basis of sex.

Women's rights activists were outraged by this ruling, which drastically reduced Title IX's scope and the original application of the law. Together with civil rights advocates who feared the extension of the ruling to race, age, and disability discrimination, they turned to Congress. The Civil Rights Restoration Act of 1987 subsequently passed by Congress effectively overturned the Supreme Court's ruling. The act provided that an entity's receipt of federal funding mandated compliance with the four civil rights laws in *all* of the entity's programs and activities, not just those that received the federal funding. Although President Ronald Reagan vetoed the bill, Congress voted to override his veto, restoring the broader coverage that had been available under the law prior to the *Grove City College* decision.

Title IX has mandated equal opportunity in the previously all-male bastion of school athletics. Before Title IX was passed in 1972, female college athletes received only 2 percent of the overall athletic budgets.[39] From 1972 to 2001, the percentage of female high school athletes went from 7.4 percent to 41.5 percent.[40] Title IX has also opened inroads for girls and women to traditionally male-dominated areas of education as well, such as math and science. It has also been used to address sexual harassment in education.[41] There are significant inherent limitations on Title IX's impact, however. The statutory penalty for noncompliance is only the withdrawal of federal funding. And Title IX applies only to schools that receive federal funding, which leaves private schools, and local and state educational programs that don't receive federal funds, free from its prohibition of sex-based discrimination.

Historically, certain explicitly discriminatory laws that were passed to protect women were considered beneficial to women. While in 1905 the Supreme Court struck down a law in New York limiting the work hours of laborers to ten hours per day, in 1908 the court upheld a law in Oregon limiting the work hours of women to ten hours per day. The court found in the laborers' case, *Lochner v. New York*, that a ten-hour limit on work hours was an impermissible interference with the right to contract freely for labor,[42] but qualified this right for women in *Muller v. Oregon* on the grounds that "women's physical structure, and the functions she performs in consequence thereof, justify special legislation restricting or qualifying the conditions under which she should be permitted to toil."[43] In the *Muller* decision, Justice David Brewer highlighted "the performance of maternal functions" and the "burdens of motherhood," noting that "as healthy mothers are essential to vigorous offspring, the physical well-being of woman becomes an object of public interest and care in order to preserve the strength and vigor of the race."[44]

The plaintiff in *Muller* was Curt Muller, the owner of a laundry business in Portland, Oregon, who had been convicted for requiring Emma Gotcher, a female employee, to work more than ten hours on September 4, 1905. He was convicted under the law and fined $10. *Lochner* had been recently decided by the Supreme Court, and Muller appealed his conviction with financial backing from the Laundry Owners' Association on the grounds that the law in Oregon discriminated against women by interfering with the contract rights that had just been upheld by the court. When the court's decision upholding the ten-hour limitation was reported in the *Oregonian*, among the headlines were "Federal Supreme Court Declares Women's Right of Contract May Be Restricted in the Interest of the General Public" and "Safeguard Human Race."[45] Brought by a woman's employer and supported by his trade association, this case challenging a protective law as discriminating against women was hardly emblematic of women's equality and empowerment on either side. Indeed, in his judgment upholding the law, Justice Brewer noted the weakness of women and "the fact that woman has always been dependent upon man."[46]

In 1974, the Supreme Court upheld a property tax exemption in Florida for widows that did not apply to widowers. In this case, *Kahn v. Shevin*, the governmental purpose identified was the reduction of disparity between the economic capabilities of men and women.[47] Citing the 1972 statistic that women made only 57 cents for every dollar made by men, Justice Douglas found that the law was substantially related to this purpose. A series of cases have followed, including cases brought by men challenging benefits exclusively or preferentially for women as discriminatory against men. In *Weinberger v. Wiesenfeld*, a 1975 case, the Supreme Court struck down a provision of the Social Security Act which allowed widows but not widowers to collect special benefits while caring for minor children. The court found the provision to be a constitutional violation of the rights of men under the Equal Protection Clause.[48] Much of the case law circles around the tension between support for protective measures recognizing the disadvantage generally faced by women, on the one hand, and the demand for equal treatment between men and women, on the other, to ensure that similarly situated men are treated the same as women.

Very little of the discussion in these cases follows the rationale articulated in *Kahn*—a rationale for affirmative action, meaning the adoption of remedial measures to address past discrimination against women, rather than the rationale for protectionism, meaning the adoption of protective measures based on a perceived inherent need that women have for special protection. In *Califano v. Webster*, the Supreme Court in 1977 upheld a pension law benefiting women by allowing them to exclude more low-earning years from the calculation of their pensions than men. In its decision, the court recognized that reduction of economic disparity between women and men caused by the long history of discrimination against women was an important governmental objective.[49] Yet in *Califano v. Goldfarb*, decided the same year, the Supreme Court struck down a pension law that treated death benefits differently on the basis of sex, automatically paying benefits to widows while paying benefits to widowers only if they were receiving at least half of their support from their wives. In this case, the court debated whether the equal protection analysis should focus on discrimination against the male widowers or against their deceased wives, concluding that the congressional intent was to aid widows, "coupled with the presumption that wives are usually dependent."[50] This presumption did not justify, according to the court, sex-based discrimination in the distribution of employment-related benefits.

The early protectionist legislation limiting women's right to work in Oregon, upheld in the *Muller* case, was not necessarily in the best interests of women, and served other interests equally or more. The state expressed an interest in preserving healthy reproduction, and the plaintiff had an interest in the freedom of contract that allowed him to contract workers for more than ten hours a day. Over time, the law took a different approach, shifting into the equal protection framework of analysis that is currently in force. This approach has not always been driven by the best interests of women either, as evidenced by the fact that one of its landmark cases is about the equal rights of young men to buy beer. Rather than championing any particular interest, such as healthy reproduction or freedom of contract, the case law has focused increasingly on the playing field rather than the players. In this context, the rights and entitlements of men are treated the same way as the rights and entitlements of women in discrimination cases. Discrimination against women is seen as equivalent to discrimination against men, with only a few dissenting comments by a few justices, and the goal is to level the playing field.

The entrenched historical inequality between the sexes cannot be erased by the creation of a level playing field because the players themselves are at two different levels. While it is easy for the Supreme Court to strike down some of the barriers women face, such as admission to

VMI or The Citadel, it is difficult for the Supreme Court to promote equality in an affirmative sense. Measures designed to redress discrimination by giving women more, such as the widow's pension in the *Kahn* case, inherently treat women and men differently, recognizing the different situations they are in. However, the stricter the scrutiny in equal protection analysis, the more difficult it is to treat women differently from men. Treating women and men as equal classes, subject to equal treatment, may level the playing field and help a few players who already have what they need to compete. But for the vast majority of women who have substantially less to begin with than men, a level playing field will serve only to keep them at the same lower level.

The jurisprudence to date on explicit distinctions drawn between women and men in the law is convoluted. It reflects differing lines of argument in differing schools of thought, which makes finding coherence challenging. While the Supreme Court has used the Equal Protection Clause of the Fourteenth Amendment to open some doors to some women, the court has not consistently recognized the realization of actual equality between women and men as the end goal. An Equal Rights Amendment that establishes this goal as a matter of constitutional right could go well beyond the limits of the Fourteenth Amendment by facilitating the use of the law to *promote* sex equality as well as to end discrimination against women.

# THE NEW ERA

A young girl sits on her father's shoulders during a rally in support of the Equal Rights Amendment in Dubuque, Iowa, ca. 1979. (Courtesy of the Iowa Women's Archives, University of Iowa Libraries, Iowa City)

Most Americans believe that women and men should have equal rights, and most also believe that the Constitution should guarantee these rights. In fact, according to a 2001 poll, nearly three out of every four Americans polled mistakenly believed that the Constitution already includes this guarantee.[1] The ERA was passed by Congress in 1972, but it is not in the Constitution. By the 1982 deadline for ratification, which had been extended in 1978, thirty-five states had ratified the ERA, just three states short of the thirty-eight needed for a constitutional amendment.

One current approach, led by Senator Benjamin Cardin,

proposes the removal by Congress of the ten-year deadline for ratification of the ERA, to enable ratification by the three additional states needed. The legal issues arising from this approach include whether Congress has the power to change the deadline after it has expired, and whether it can be changed by a majority vote. If the legislation is passed and upheld by the Supreme Court, only three more state ratifications could put the ERA in the Constitution. If unsuccessful, the process of ratification would have to begin all over again.

Beginning again without a deadline is the other approach. Over the course of the past thirty years, Representative Carolyn Maloney and Senator Edward Kennedy were longtime sponsors of the ERA, reintroducing it in every session of Congress. More recently, Senator Robert Menendez has sponsored the ERA in the Senate, and in the House, Representative Maloney has introduced a new ERA with a sentence explicitly mentioning women, drawn from the text originally drafted by Alice Paul in 1923, followed by the text of the ERA passed in 1972.

Some advocates are also promoting state ERAs, which would advance constitutional sex equality rights incrementally, state by state, and reinforce efforts to support a federal ERA.

**The ERA Coalition was formed in 2014 to bring organizations and individuals together to support any and all efforts to put equal rights for women into the Constitution, both at the state and the federal level (www.eracoalition.org).**

Since 1982, when the extended deadline for ratification of the Equal Rights Amendment expired, the ERA has been reintroduced in every session of Congress. A two-thirds vote of both the House and Senate would be required to send the ERA to the states, where after ratification by thirty-eight states, it would become part of the Constitution. A poll in 2001 found that 96 percent of Americans believed that women and men should have equal rights, and 88 percent believed that the Constitution should guarantee these equal rights. However, nearly three-quarters of the Americans polled—72 percent—mistakenly believed that the Constitution already includes this guarantee.[2] No doubt some of these people are thinking of the Fourteenth Amendment and its Equal Protection Clause as that guarantee. As the cases in this book illustrate, however, the Equal Protection Clause has not effectively protected women from pay inequity, pregnancy discrimination, gender-based violence, and other forms of sex discrimination. And it has not effectively promoted equality between women and men.

The first ERA introduced in 1923 by Alice Paul read as follows:

> Men and women shall have equal rights throughout the United States and every place subject to its jurisdiction. Congress shall have power to enforce this article by appropriate legislation.

By the time the ERA first came to a vote in Congress in 1946, the language had evolved into more or less the form in which it was ultimately passed in 1972:

> Equality of rights under the law shall not be denied or abridged by the United States or any State on account of sex. The Congress shall have the power to enforce, by appropriate legislation, the provisions of this article.

Much debate concerned the potential impact of the ERA on protectionist legislation, and in 1950, Senator Carl Hayden proposed additional language to qualify the ERA so that it would not undermine
this legislation. Called the Hayden rider, this language stated: "The
provisions of this article shall not be construed to impair any rights,
benefits, or exemptions conferred by law upon persons of the female
sex." Many proponents of the ERA opposed the Hayden rider, including the one woman serving in the Senate at the time, Margaret Chase
Smith of Maine. Nevertheless, with the rider, the ERA passed the Senate by a two-thirds majority twice in the 1950s.

The Senate continued to debate the ERA, and opposition to the
Hayden rider prevailed in 1964, when the Senate Judiciary Committee's report stated that the rider was unacceptable to women's rights
advocates. "It is under the guise of so-called 'rights' or 'benefits,'" the
report explained, "that women have been treated unequally and denied
opportunities which are available to men." When the ERA passed both
houses of Congress, it was without qualification. When it came to the
floor of the House of Representatives in October 1971, it was passed by
a bipartisan vote of 354–23. In March 1972, the Senate approved the
House version of the ERA by a bipartisan vote of 84–8. The Joint Resolution passed by Congress proposing the Equal Rights Amendment
included a preamble with the following language:

> The following article is proposed as an amendment to the Con-
> stitution of the United States, which shall be valid to all intents
> and purposes as part of the Constitution when ratified by the
> legislatures of three-fourths of the several States within seven
> years of its submission by the Congress:

As noted before, this seven-year deadline was extended to just over ten
years in 1978, but by the expiration of the deadline on June 30, 1982,
the ERA remained three states short of the thirty-eight states needed to
put it into the Constitution.

Article V of the Constitution, which defines the constitutional
amendment process, makes no mention of time limits for ratification. Prior to passage of the Eighteenth Amendment, there were no

deadlines for ratification by states in any constitutional amendments passed by Congress. The Eighteenth Amendment, which prohibited the production, transport, and sale of alcohol in the United States, was passed in 1917. Future president Warren Harding, then a senator from Ohio, proposed the seven-year deadline for ratification, reportedly as a way of allowing himself and others to support the amendment, thus gaining favor from Prohibition advocates, while assuming that it would ultimately fail for lack of ratification by states within the time limit. This political calculation backfired when the amendment was ratified by three-quarters of the states and became effective just thirteen months after its passage. The Eighteenth Amendment was subsequently repealed in 1933, even more quickly than it had been adopted, when states ratified the Twenty-First Amendment less than ten months after it was passed by Congress.

The seven-year deadline had no impact on either the ratification or the annulment of Prohibition, but ironically, it served as a precedent for future amendments. All but two of the constitutional amendments passed by Congress since the Eighteenth Amendment have included a seven-year ratification deadline. The two exceptions were the Nineteenth Amendment on women's suffrage, passed in 1919 without a deadline and ratified in 1920 just over a year later, and the Child Labor Amendment, which was passed in 1924 but never ratified and generally considered unnecessary in light of subsequent congressional legislation upheld as constitutional by the Supreme Court. While most recent amendments to the Constitution have been ratified within a few years of their passage by Congress, the Twenty-Seventh Amendment, called the Madison Amendment because it was introduced by James Madison in 1789, was finally ratified in 1992, more than two hundred years after its passage by Congress. This amendment delays salary increases passed by Congress for its own members from taking effect until after a subsequent public election.

The bills currently pending in Congress that deal with the Equal Rights Amendment represent two different approaches to securing its adoption, one inspired by the ratification of the Madison Amendment in 1992. This approach, known as the "three-state strategy," relies on the fact that the seven-year time frame for ratification of the ERA was

Jimmy Carter signs a bill extending the ratification deadline for the Equal Rights Amendment, October 20, 1978. (Carter White House Photographs Collection, Jimmy Carter Library, Atlanta, GA)

included in the text of the preamble rather than the text of the amendment itself. When it became clear in the late 1970s that the number of states needed for ratification would not be reached by the end of seven years, Representative Elizabeth Holtzman of New York sponsored a bill that extended the deadline to ten years and three months, setting it to expire before the 1982 election. It was signed by President Jimmy Carter in 1978, with a disclaimer indicating the uncertainty over whether his signature was in fact necessary. Advocates of the three-state strategy take the view that the time limit can again be amended, or eliminated, by congressional legislation. In May 2013, Senator Cardin from Maryland introduced S.J. Res. 15 to remove the deadline for ratification of the ERA. A companion bill in the House of Representatives, H.J. Res. 113, is sponsored by Representative Jackie Speier from California.

When, in 1978, the Holtzman bill to amend the time frame for ERA ratification was debated in Congress, one of the proposals made and rejected in committee was that the bill should be passed by a two-thirds supermajority rather than a simple majority. The argument for this proposal was that the preamble, as well as the amendment, had been approved in 1972 by a two-thirds vote, as required by the Article V amendment process. This issue came up again when the bill went to the floor for a vote, but an amendment requiring a two-thirds vote was defeated. The deadline extension passed the House of Representatives by a vote of 233–189, and the Senate a few months later by a vote of 60–36.

The congressional legislation extending the deadline for ratification of the ERA was challenged in an Idaho federal district court by the states of Idaho and Arizona and some individual legislators from the state of Washington, who argued that Washington's ratification of the ERA was null and void, as it had been conditional on full ratification by three-fourths of the states within the seven-year time frame. Looking to Article V of the Constitution, which governs the passage and ratification of amendments, the district court's chief judge Marion Callister rejected the argument that the power of Congress to control the amendment process is not subject to judicial review, characterizing the suggestion that the courts should have no role in the process as "completely counter to the intentions of the founding fathers."[3] However, Judge Callister noted that Congress did have the power to determine the "mode of ratification," meaning making a choice between state legislatures, which is how all but one amendment to date have been considered, and state conventions, an alternative provided for by Article V that has been used once, for the repeal of Prohibition. In giving Congress this power, the judge reasoned, Article V implicitly gave Congress the power to set a time frame for ratification.[4]

Judge Callister cited a Supreme Court case, *Dillon v. Gloss*, which had held, with regard to the Eighteenth Amendment—the first amendment to have a time frame—that a deadline was permissible, i.e., that Article V of the Constitution did not *require* Congress to keep a proposed amendment "open to ratification for all time."[5] Characterizing the process of ratification as "succeeding steps in a single endeavor," the Supreme Court had suggested a natural inference "that they are not to be widely separated in time."[6] The court had gone even further, saying, "[T]here is a fair implication that it must be sufficiently contemporaneous in that number of States to reflect the will of the people in all sections at relatively the same period, which of course ratification scattered through a long series of years would not do."[7]

Based on this Supreme Court decision, Judge Callister concluded: "Whether a definite period for ratification shall be fixed so that all may know what it is and speculation on what is a reasonable time may be avoided, is, in our opinion, a matter of detail which Congress may determine as an incident of its power to designate the mode of ratification."[8] The judge questioned, however, whether Congress, under its power to propose the mode of amendment ratification, had the power to change its proposal once made, and if so, whether that could be done by less than a two-thirds majority. Citing Supreme Court jurisprudence, Judge Callister noted that if no deadline had initially been established for an amendment, Congress would retain its authority to set one. He affirmed that what the time frame itself was, rested entirely within the province of Congress, not subject to court review. However, Judge Callister held that once a time frame was established, it could not be changed. The determination of the time frame, according to his decision, "becomes an integral part of the proposed mode of ratification" and changing it would be like changing the mode of ratification from state legislatures to state conventions. "Once the proposal is made," Judge Callister held, "Congress is not at liberty to change it."[9]

The judge stated further that in any event, the extension of the time frame for the ERA was "in violation of the constitutional requirement that Congress act by two-thirds of both Houses when exercising its article V powers."[10] He rejected the argument that, because it was in the preamble rather than the text of the amendment itself, the time frame could be changed by Congress pursuant to its power under Article I, setting forth the powers of Congress generally, rather than Article V, setting forth the amendment process. It was under Article V, Judge Callister held, that Congress had the power to propose the text of an amendment and the power to propose its mode of ratification, including the time frame. In conclusion, the judge summarized his decision as follows:

> While Congress is not required to set a time period in advance
> of the requisite number of states acting to ratify, if it chooses to

do so to remove uncertainty regarding the question, it cannot thereafter remove that certainty by changing the time period. In addition, since it is clear that Congress must act by a two-thirds concurrence of both Houses when acting pursuant to its authority under article V, and because the extension resolution was enacted by only a simple majority, the extension resolution is an unconstitutional exercise of congressional authority under article V.[11]

The other issue addressed by the Idaho court was the vote of the Idaho legislature in 1978 to rescind its ratification of the ERA, which had been voted for by the state in 1972 just after Congress passed the ERA. Over the course of the decade, five states voted to rescind their ratification of the ERA.[12] In considering this issue, Judge Callister outlined three alternative approaches: (i) The state's power to accept or reject the amendment can be exercised once, and its decision cannot later be modified; (ii) the state has only the power to ratify an amendment, hence only acts of ratification are relevant, and neither prior rejection nor subsequent rescission has any impact on ratification; and (iii) all acts of rejection, ratification, and rescission should be recognized so long as any subsequent rescission is prior to the ratification of the amendment by three-fourths of the states, at which point the amendment becomes part of the Constitution and state ratification can no longer be rescinded.[13]

Judge Callister adopted this third approach on the theory that allowing subsequent acts of rescission "would promote the democratic ideal by giving a truer picture of the people's will as of the time three-fourths of the states have acted in affirming the amendment." Either of the other approaches would, in the court's estimation, "permit an amendment to be ratified by a technicality—where clearly one is not intended—and not because there is really a considered consensus supporting the amendment which is the avowed purpose of the amendment procedure."[14] The judge reviewed the history of several other amendments where states changed their votes, citing the Fifteenth Amendment as well as the Nineteenth Amendment, in which cases the national government waited for additional ratifications before promulgating the amendments. For these reasons, the judge held that "a rescission of a prior ratification must be recognized if it occurs prior to unrescinded ratification by three-fourths of the states."[15]

The Idaho court's decision was appealed, and the Supreme Court initially agreed to hear the appeal. However, after the extended ratification deadline for the ERA expired in 1982, the case became moot. The Supreme Court vacated the district court's decision and remanded the case to the lower court with instructions to dismiss it.[16] The Idaho court's decision is therefore null and void. If the three-state legislation sponsored by Senator Cardin and Representative Speier should pass, removing the deadline for ratification, and if Illinois, Virginia, Florida, and/or other states now ratify the ERA, there would likely be litigation over the validity of the process. Although the Idaho court's decision would have no bearing on the outcome of any future litigation, the arguments made on both sides would be raised again and would all be adjudicated anew: whether Congress has the power to remove the ratification deadline; if so, whether it can be done by a simple majority vote rather than two-thirds; and whether the rescission by five states of their ratification is valid. Judge Callister, a Mormon, had denied a request to recuse himself from the case because of a possible conflict of interest.[17] Depending on the court, the decision could come out either way, as there are viable legal arguments on both sides of all these issues.

In practical political terms, the argument for the three-state strategy is that it would be much easier to get a majority vote of Congress than the two-thirds needed for an amendment, and it would be much easier to get three additional states to ratify the ERA rather than starting all over, with ratification by thirty-eight states needed. Illinois, Florida, and Virginia are often mentioned as three states that might ratify the ERA. In 2003, the Illinois House of Representatives voted to ratify the ERA, and in May 2014, the Illinois Senate voted to ratify it. Three times—in 2011, 2012, and 2014—the Virginia Senate passed a joint resolution to ratify the ERA. ERA ratification bills have been introduced in six of the other so-called "unratified" states—Arizona, Arkansas, Mississippi, Missouri, Nevada, and Oklahoma—since the three-state strategy was developed in 1994, and many of these bills have seen legislative action in committee. The other six states that have not ratified the ERA are: Alabama, Georgia, Louisiana, North Carolina, South Carolina, and Utah. If three of these states ratify the ERA, and if the federal legislation removing the deadline is challenged, as it almost certainly would be, the decision on whether the Constitution will have an Equal Rights Amendment will ultimately be made by the Supreme Court.

For those who support the three-state strategy, this is a gamble worth taking. If Congress has the power to set a deadline, arguably Congress has the power to remove it. The text of the preamble to the amendment, which governs only the process and does not form part of the amendment itself, can arguably be changed by a majority vote if it is only the text of the amendment that is found to require a two-thirds vote. The argument that state rescissions are invalid is supported by the fact that in promulgating the Fourteenth Amendment in 1868, Congress listed as ratifying states both states which had rescinded their ratifications and states which had first rejected and then ratified the amendment.[18] If successful, the three-state strategy could be an effective way to build on the tremendous amount of work that has already been done to put the ERA into the Constitution. If unsuccessful, however, the process of ratification would have to begin all over again.

Beginning again without a deadline is the other approach, supported by those who are concerned that the three-state strategy will be rejected by the Supreme Court if it fails on any of the legal arguments that must be made for its validity. There are currently two different Equal Rights Amendment texts pending in bills before Congress. One is the 1972 ERA, which contains the same text as the ERA passed in 1972 and which has been reintroduced in every session of Congress since the expiration of the ratification deadline in 1982. In 1983, it was voted out of committee in the House of Representatives for a vote on the floor, which fell six votes short of the two-thirds needed for a constitutional amendment. Since then, the ERA has not once been voted on in either the House or the Senate. In the Senate, for more than twenty years the ERA bill was sponsored by Senator Edward Kennedy. The same bill currently pending in the Senate is sponsored by Senator

Robert Menendez from New Jersey. Over the past thirty years there has not been a single congressional hearing on the ERA.

In the House of Representatives, Carolyn Maloney has been the principal sponsor of the ERA for fifteen years. In 2013, Representative Maloney introduced the "new ERA," H.J. Res. 56, which is the 1972 ERA text with an additional sentence at the beginning. It reads:

> **Women shall have equal rights in the United States and every place subject to its jurisdiction.** Equality of rights under the law shall not be denied or abridged by the United States or by any State on account of sex.

The new language is an affirmative statement of rights that puts "women" into the Constitution. It helps clarify that the purpose of the amendment is particularly to address the historical discrimination against women referred to in the jurisprudence. If the amendment process is to begin all over again, the "new ERA" takes this opportunity to build on the language of the 1972 ERA in an effort to ensure that the limitations on the Fourteenth Amendment as it has been interpreted are not placed on the ERA as well. While "new," the language of Representative Maloney's bill draws heavily from the text originally drafted by Alice Paul in 1923, setting forth a substantive right to sex equality as a vision for the future. Another new feature of the language introduced by Representative Maloney is that it mentions states, as well as Congress, as having the power to enforce the amendment by appropriate legislation.

Supportive members of Congress, as well as the ERA advocates in the women's movement, generally support all strategies for adoption of the ERA, while some focus on one approach more than the other. There are also advocates focusing on state ERAs, including an initiative that has placed the ERA on the November 2014 ballot in Oregon.[19] State ERAs are a way of incrementally advancing, state by state, constitutional protection of women and promotion of sex equality. The promotion of state ERAs is also creating forces on the ground, state by state, that reinforce efforts to support a federal ERA, whether by way of a three-state strategy or a new ERA.

The ERA Coalition was formed in 2014 to bring organizations and individuals together to support any and all of the efforts to put equal rights for women into the Constitution, both at the state and the federal levels. In the years since the ERA campaign of the 1970s, the Four-teenth Amendment, which was then seen as a potential alternative source of legal protection, has been interpreted by the Supreme Court in ways that fail to effectively address sex discrimination. In many ways, the same failings have plagued efforts to address race discrimi-nation as well: the state action requirement, the need to prove intent to discriminate, and the unwillingness otherwise to redress the impact on its victims, no matter how overwhelming the evidence of systemic discrimination. Also of common concern is the treatment of "suspect classifications" as though they already enjoyed equality, and the failure of equal protection analysis under the Fourteenth Amendment to take into account the fact that equal treatment of unequally situated people only perpetuates inequality, leaving them unequally situated.

In the early decades of the twentieth century, the first wave of cam-paigning for the ERA, when it was introduced in 1923, was plagued by opposition from women as well as men. Fearing that it would un-dermine legislation designed to protect women from harsh working conditions, these women did not focus on the underlying assumptions of inferiority represented by the laws. Now there is greater understand-ing that it is the workplace, not the law, that has to be changed to meet the needs of women and men equally rather than meeting the needs of men and using measures such as protectionist legislation to meet the needs of women.

In the second wave of ERA campaigning, which came so close to success in the 1970s and early 1980s, again some women were seen as opposing the ERA. Phyllis Schlafly and her STOP ERA campaign created a media circus, where divisions among women were promoted and highlighted and exploited, if not fabricated, by those with eco-nomic and political interests in opposing the ERA. The fears of that time, which were used to fuel the anti-ERA campaign, are largely gone now. The fight over abortion, still controversial, is being played out elsewhere following the landmark *Roe v. Wade* decision in 1973, when the Supreme Court decided that a woman's decision to have an abortion fell within the right to privacy under the Due Process Clause of the Fourteenth Amendment. The right to choose abortion is already protected by the Constitution.

To the extent that concern over the financial cost of equality for women was a factor in the ERA's defeat in 1982, there is a growing recognition around the world that gender equality is not only the *right* thing to do but that it's also the *smart* thing to do. Empowering women has a documented impact on the health and welfare of their families and communities, with significant implications for the national economy. Many of the hidden costs of sex discrimination, such as the financial cost of domestic violence, may not have been taken into account by the opposition to the last campaign for the ERA. Moreover, there are more women in higher positions, politically and economically, than ever before who "hold these truths to be self-evident," that all men *and women* are created equal with certain inalienable rights. No matter what their race, class, political party, or economic status, women all have much to gain from the ERA. And the "gender gap" has come to refer not only to wage differentials but also to voting differentials that give women political power to insist that their congressional representatives, regardless of political affiliation, support the inclusion of their rights in the Constitution. This is truly a bipartisan issue. The new campaign for the ERA is also a campaign by women *and men*, for women *and men*, with recognition that sex equality is beneficial to men as well as women.

The way our Constitution works, we cannot say with certainty what exactly the ERA will or won't do for women who are hoping it will end sex discrimination. It is for Congress and state legislatures to pass laws, and for courts to interpret them. What we can say with certainty is that the ERA will give the courts a new standard, a clear and strong statement of sex equality. It will ensure that no Supreme Court justice can ever again say, as Justice Scalia has done, that the Constitution does not prohibit discrimination against women.

State ERAs have been passed in twenty-two states.[20] Most of these state constitutional amendments were passed in the 1970s, while the campaign for the federal ERA was in full swing. For women in these states, the ERA offers an additional avenue of recourse with widely varying results, not only because of the courts but also because the language of these ERAs varies. In some states, such as Rhode Island and Florida, the courts have closely tracked the jurisprudence of the Fourteenth Amendment. In other states, such as Colorado, New Mexico, Pennsylvania, and Washington, the courts have gone beyond the Fourteenth Amendment to advance women's equality. In both Washington and Illinois, the state supreme courts explicitly noted that the passage of the ERA was intended to expand the scope of existing constitutional protection.[21] And in Colorado, the state supreme court held that excluding the costs of normal pregnancy care from otherwise comprehensive insurance coverage constitutes sex discrimination in violation of the Colorado ERA.[22]

Equal rights for women are also in some form or another included in most constitutions around the world. Yet severe forms of sex discrimination persist in many of these countries, where the language of the law is far from reality. The law is a starting point, not an end point. But having sex equality language in the Constitution is a critical step that is missing in the United States. Compounded by the U.S. failure to ratify the United Nations Convention on the Elimination of All Forms of Discrimination Against Women (CEDAW), it is crippling efforts by the United States to claim leadership on women's rights around the world.

The Fourteenth Amendment could have been interpreted differently as early as the 1880s, soon after its adoption, and the course of legal history would have been very different. Following the Supreme Court's *Gilbert* decision in 1976, which denied pregnant women protection under the Fourteenth Amendment's Equal Protection Clause, Congress passed the Pregnancy Discrimination Act, effectively overruling the Supreme Court's decision in that case. In other cases, however, such as *Morrison*, where the Supreme Court struck down the private right of action in the Violence Against Women Act as unconstitutional, the only remedy is to change the Constitution. This book should clarify not only that equal rights are *not* in the Constitution but also that they *need* to be there and that they will make a meaningful difference in the daily lives of women and girls across the country.

The power of constitutional democracy is its ability to evolve and respond to needs that it has not to date adequately addressed. The structure is designed to make our imperfect union ever more perfect. The ERA will give women a new lease on life under the law, and it will let the Supreme Court know, when it interprets the ERA, that the intent in passing it was to clarify that equal *means* equal. Women's rights are not merely procedural. They are substantive—in other words, *real.* A statement of the fundamental right to sex equality is needed in the Constitution to ensure that the laws in the United States allow women equal enjoyment of life, liberty, and the pursuit of happiness. Let our generation end the debate over whether women and men are equal. The time for the ERA is now.

(Jennifer Macleod)

# Equal Rights Amendment Texts
# and Related Legislation

ERA drafted by Alice Paul and introduced in Congress in 1923:
*Men and women shall have equal rights throughout the
United States and every place subject to its jurisdiction.*

---

ERA passed in 1972 (reintroduced by Senator
Robert Menendez in 2013 as S.J. Res. 10):
*Section 1. Equality of rights under the law shall not be denied or abridged by
the United States or by any state on account of sex.*
*Section 2. The Congress shall have the power to enforce, by appropriate
legislation, the provisions of this article.*
*Section 3. This amendment shall take effect two years after the date of
ratification.*

---

New ERA introduced by Representative Carolyn
Maloney in 2013 (H.J. Res. 56):
*Section 1. Women shall have equal rights in the United States and every
place subject to its jurisdiction. Equality of rights under the law shall not
be denied or abridged by the United States or by any State on account
of sex.*
*Section 2. Congress and the several States shall have the power to enforce, by
appropriate legislation, the provisions of this article.*
*Section 3. This amendment shall take effect two years after the date of
ratification.*

---

"3-State Strategy" Legislation introduced by Senator Benjamin Cardin in 2013 (S.J. Res. 15) and Representative Jackie Speier (H.J. Res. 113)

## JOINT RESOLUTION
*Removing the deadline for the ratification of the Equal Rights Amendment.*

*Resolved by the Senate and House of Representatives of the United States of America in Congress assembled, That notwithstanding any time limit contained in House Joint Resolution 208, 92d Congress, as agreed to in the Senate on March 22, 1972, the article of amendment proposed to the States in that joint resolution shall be valid to all intents and purposes as part of the Constitution whenever ratified by the legislatures of three-fourths of the several States.*

# APPENDIX 2

# Websites for Action and Further Reading

## WEBSITES

ERA Coalition: www.eracoalition.org

Alice Paul Institute: www.alicepaul.org

Representative Carolyn Maloney's (D-NY) ERA page: maloney.house .gov/issue/equal-rights-amendment

Senator Ben Cardin's (D-MD) ERA page: www.cardin.senate.gov /eracosponsor

Equality 4 Women: www.equality4women.org

The Equal Rights Amendment, www.equalrightsamendment.org

ERA Education Project: www.ERAeducationproject.com

United 4 Equality: www.united4equality.org

VoteERA.org: www.voteera.org

We Are Woman: www.wearewoman.us

2PassERA.org: www.2passera.org

## FACEBOOK

ERA Coalition: www.facebook.com/ERAcoalition

Boys and Men for the ERA: www.facebook.com/BoysAndMenFor TheERA

ERA Action: www.facebook.com/ERAAction

ERA Once and For All: www.facebook.com/ERAonceandforall

Equal Rights Amendment: www.facebook.com/ERAusa

Women Matter Use Your Power: www.facebook.com/womenmatter useyourpower

## BOOKS

Berry, Mary Frances. *Why ERA Failed: Politics, Women's Rights, and the Amending Process of the Constitution.* Bloomington: Indiana University Press, 1988.

Brown, Barbara A., et al. *Women's Rights and the Law: The Impact of the ERA on State Laws.* New York; Praeger, 1977.

Eisler, Riane Tennenhaus. *The Equal Rights Handbook: What ERA Means to Your Life, Your Rights, and the Future.* New York: Avon Books, 1978.

Hoff-Wilson, Joan, ed. *Rights of Passage: The Past and Future of the ERA.* Bloomington: Indiana University Press, 1986.

Johnson, Sonia. *From Housewife to Heretic.* New York: Doubleday, 1981.

MacKinnon, Catharine A. *Sex Equality,* 2nd ed. New York: Foundation Press, 2007.

Mansbridge, Jane J. *Why We Lost the ERA.* Chicago: University of Chicago Press, 1986.

Mathews, Donald G., and Jane Sherron De Hart. *Sex, Gender, and the Politics of ERA: A State and the Nation.* New York: Oxford University Press, 1990.

## ARTICLES

Brown, Barbara A., Thomas I. Emerson, Gail Falk, and Ann E. Freedman. "The Equal Rights Amendment: A Constitutional Basis for Equal Rights for Women." *Yale Law Journal* 80, no. 5 (1971): 871–985.

Dow, Phyllis A. "Sexual Equality, the ERA and the Court—A Tale of Two Failures." *New Mexico Law Review* 13, no. 1 (Winter 1983): 53–97.

Ginsburg, Ruth Bader. "Sexual Equality Under the Fourteenth and Equal Rights Amendments," *Washington University Law Review* 1979, no. 1: *Symposium: The Quest for Equality* (1979): 161–78.

Held, Allison L., Sheryl L. Herndon, and Danielle M. Stager. "The Equal Rights Amendment: Why the ERA Remains Legally Viable and Properly Before the States." *William and Mary Journal of Women and the Law* 3, no. 1 (Spring 1997): 113–36.

Kalfus, Mason. "Why Time Limits on the Ratification of Constitutional Amendments Violate Article V." *University of Chicago Law Review* 66, no. 2 (Spring 1999).

MacKinnon, Catharine A. "Toward a Renewed Equal Rights Amendment: Now More Than Ever." *Harvard Journal of Law & Gender* 37 (2014): 569–79.

Mayeri, Serena. "A New E.R.A. or a New Era? Amendment Advocacy and the Reconstitution of Feminism." *Northwestern University Law Review* 103, no. 3 (2009): 1223–301.

Neale, Thomas H. "The Proposed Equal Rights Amendment: Contemporary Ratification Issues." Congressional Research Service, February 28, 2013, updated April 8, 2014.

Sullivan, Kathleen M. "Constitutionalizing Women's Equality." *California Law Review* 90, no. 3 (May 2002): 735–64.

Wharton, Linda J. "State Equal Rights Amendments Revisited: Evaluating Their Effectiveness in Advancing Protection Against Sex Discrimination." *Rutgers Law Journal* 36, no. 4 (2006): 1201–93.

# The First National Women's Conference, Houston 1977

From November 18 to 21, 1977, twenty thousand people gathered in Houston for the First National Women's Conference. The conference had been authorized and financed by Congress, pursuant to legislation sponsored by Representative Bella Abzug of New York, Public Law 94-167, which called on the Conference to:

"recognize the contributions of women to the development of our country;

"assess the progress that has been made to date by both the private and public sectors in promoting equality between men and women in all aspects of life in the United States;

"assess the role of women in economic, social, cultural, and political development;

"assess the participation in efforts aimed at the development of friendly relations and cooperation among nations and to the strengthening of world peace;

"identify the barriers that prevent women from participating fully and equally in all aspects of national life and develop recommendations for means by which such barriers can be removed;

"establish a timetable for the achievement of the objectives set forth in such recommendations; and

"establish a committee of the conference which will take steps

---

"The Spirit of Houston: The First National Women's Conference: An Official Report to the President, the Congress and the People of the United States. National Commission on the Observance of International Women's Year," Washington, DC, March 1978.

to provide for the convening of the second National Women's Conference . . . to evaluate the steps taken to improve the status of American women."

At the Conference, which was comprised of delegates from across the country, a National Plan of Action was adopted, consisting of a Declaration and twenty-six planks as follows:

## DECLARATION OF AMERICAN WOMEN 1977

We are here to move history forward.

We are women from every State and Territory in the Nation.

We are women of different ages, beliefs and lifestyles.

We are women of many economic, social, political, ethnic, cultural, educational and religious backgrounds.

We are married, single, widowed and divorced.

We are mothers and daughters.

We are sisters.

We speak in varied accents and languages but we share the common language and experience of American women who throughout our Nation's life have been denied the opportunities, rights, privileges and responsibilities accorded to men.

For the first time in the more than 200 years of our democracy, we are gathered in a National Women's Conference, charged under federal law to assess the status of women in our country, to measure the progress we have made, to identify the barriers that prevent us from participating fully and equally in all aspects of national life, and to make recommendations to the President and to the Congress for means by which such barriers can be removed.

We recognize the positive changes that have occurred in the lives of women since the founding of our nation. In more than a century of struggle from Seneca Falls 1848 to Houston 1977, we have progressed from being non-persons and slaves whose work and achievements were unrecognized, whose needs were ignored, and whose rights were suppressed to being citizens with freedoms and aspirations of which our ancestors could only dream.

We can vote and own property. We work in the home, in our

communities and in every occupation. We are 40 percent of the labor force. We are in the arts, sciences, professions and politics. We raise children, govern States, head businesses and institutions, climb mountains, explore the ocean depths and reach toward the moon.

Our lives no longer end with the childbearing years. Our lifespan has increased to more than 75 years. We have become a majority of the population, 51.3 percent, and by the 21st century, we shall be an even larger majority.

But despite some gains made in the past 200 years, our dream of equality is still withheld from us and millions of women still face a daily reality of discrimination, limited opportunities and economic hardship.

Man-made barriers, laws, social customs and prejudices continue to keep a majority of women in an inferior position without full control of our lives and bodies.

From infancy throughout life, in personal and public relationships, in the family, in the schools, in every occupation and profession, too often we find our individuality, our capabilities, our earning powers diminished by discriminatory practices and outmoded ideas of what a woman is, what a woman can do, and what a woman must be.

Increasingly, we are victims of crimes of violence in a culture that degrades us as sex objects and promotes pornography for profit.

We are poorer than men. And those of us who are minority women—blacks, Hispanic Americans, Native Americans, and Asian Americans—must overcome the double burden of discrimination based on race and sex.

We lack effective political and economic power. We have only minor and insignificant roles in making, interpreting and enforcing our laws, in running our political parties, businesses, unions, schools and institutions, in directing the media, in governing our country, in deciding issues of war or peace.

We do not seek special privileges, but we demand as a human right a full voice and role for women in determining the destiny of our world, our nation, our families and our individual lives.

We seek these rights for all women, whether or not they choose as individuals to use them.

We are part of a worldwide movement of women who believe that only by bringing women into full partnership with men and respecting our rights as half the human race can we hope to achieve a world in which the whole human race—men, women and children—can live in peace and security.

Based on the views of women who have met in every State and Territory in the past year, the National Plan of Action is presented to the President and the Congress as our recommendations for implementing Public Law 94-167.

We are entitled to and expect serious attention to our proposals.

We demand immediate and continuing action on our National Plan by Federal, State, public, and private institutions so that by 1985, the end of the International Decade for Women proclaimed by the United Nations, everything possible under the law will have been done to provide American women with full equality.

The rest will be up to the hearts, minds and moral consciences of men and women and what they do to make our society truly democratic and open to all.

We pledge ourselves with all the strength of our Dedication to this struggle "to form a more perfect Union."

Plank 1: Arts and Humanities
Plank 2: Battered Women
Plank 3: Business
Plank 4: Child Abuse
Plank 5: Child Care
Plank 6: Credit
Plank 7: Disabled Women
Plank 8: Education
Plank 9: Elective and Appointive Office
Plank 10: Employment
Plank 11: Equal Rights Amendment (full text follows)
Plank 12: Health
Plank 13: Homemakers
Plank 14: Insurance
Plank 15: International Affairs

Plank 16: Media
Plank 17: Minority Women
Plank 18: Offenders
Plank 19: Older Women
Plank 20: Rape
Plank 21: Reproductive Freedom
Plank 22: Rural Women
Plank 23: Sexual Preference
Plank 24: Statistics
Plank 25: Women, Welfare, and Poverty
Plank 26: Continuing Committee of the Conference

Plank 11: Equal Rights Amendment

The Equal Rights Amendment should be ratified.

**BACKGROUND:**

*Women have waited more than 200 years for the equality promised by the Declaration of Independence to all men.*

Women will not have equality in the United States unless it is guaranteed by the Constitution. In 1978, more than 200 years after the founding of this Nation, American women, 51.3 percent of the population, still are not the equals of men before the law. The rights they have are unclear and incomplete and are at the mercy of conflicting State laws and inconsistent court decisions. There is no clear standard to guide legislators in writing laws about women or to guide judges in interpreting them.

The Equal Rights Amendment has been ratified by 35 States, in which three-fourths of the U.S. population live. Approval by only three more States is needed to make the ERA part of the Constitution. Under the preamble to the amendment approved by Congress, ratification must be completed by March 22, 1979, unless Congress votes to extend that date.

Although a majority of Americans favor equal rights for women, ratification in the remaining States has been blocked by a well-organized, well-financed minority that relies on many of the same false arguments that were used to prevent women from getting the vote, namely, that ERA would destroy the family and morality. In some States, ratification has been held up by the negative votes of as few as two or three male legislators.

The Equal Rights Amendment itself is short and simple:

"Section 1: Equality of rights under the law shall not be denied or abridged by the United States or by any State on account of sex.

"Section 2: The Congress shall have the power to enforce, by appropriate legislation, the provisions of this article.

"Section 3: This amendment shall take effect two years after the date of ratification."

## WHY AN AMENDMENT IS NEEDED

The Declaration of Independence, signed in 1776, stated that "all men are created equal" and that governments derive their powers "from the consent of the governed." Women were not included in either concept. The original American Constitution of 1787 was founded on English common law, which did not recognize women as citizens or as individuals with legal rights. A woman was expected to obey her husband or nearest male kin, and if she was married, her person and her property were owned by her husband. The power of the ballot was denied to her by the States, which also denied it to Indians, slaves, the mentally unfit, and criminals.

It has been argued that the ERA is not necessary because the 14th Amendment, passed after the Civil War, guarantees that no State shall deny to "any person within its jurisdiction the equal protection of the laws."

Early court decisions made clear, however, that women were not necessarily persons under the 14th Amendment. In a famous lower court ruling in 1872, the judge in the trial of Susan B. Anthony, who was charged with committing a Federal offense because she voted in the 1872 Presidential election, stated flatly: "I have decided as a question of law . . . that under the 14th amendment, which Miss Anthony claims protects her, she was not protected in a right to vote." The judge prevented Anthony from appealing to the U.S. Supreme Court, but in the same year the high court approved an Illinois law prohibiting women from being licensed to practice law. *Bradwell v. State*, 83 U.S. 916, Wall. 130 (1872).

Since then, the Supreme Court has struck down some gender discrimination laws but has allowed others to stand, and no majority opinion has articulated sex as a "suspect" classification, like race, under the 14th Amendment. See also *Goesart v. Cleary*, 335 U.S. 464 (1948) and *Hoyt v. Florida*, 368 U.S. 57 ('96'). Indeed, the first time sex classifications were struck down by the Supreme Court was as recently as 1971. *Reed v. Reed*, 404 U.S. 71 (1971).

If the courts had interpreted sex classifications by the same strict scrutiny standard as race classifications under the 14th Amendment, the need for a constitutional amendment would have been less compelling. When the court does consider a particular basis of classification— such as race—to be suspect, it triggers a "compelling State interest" standard of judicial review which, as a practical matter, the State can rarely, if ever, satisfy. Thus, under constitutional challenges, race-based classifications are often struck down as unconstitutional.

Just as women were not included under the 14th Amendment, they were also omitted from the 15th Amendment, which enfranchised former slaves, but males only. This exclusion from coverage resulted in a century-long struggle that ended with approval of the 19th Amendment guaranteeing women the right to vote.

Aside from the fact that women have been subjected to varying, inconsistent, and often unfavorable decisions under the 14th Amendment, the Equal Rights Amendment is a more immediate and effective remedy to sex discrimination in Federal and State laws than a case-by-case interpretation under the 14th Amendment could ever be. The critical distinction is that under the ERA, sex is a prohibited classification, not a classification that is subject to some level of judicial review and that, therefore, may or may not be sustained.

## WHAT THE ERA WILL DO

In interpreting the ERA, the courts can be expected to rely on the legislative history as expressed in the majority report of the Senate Judiciary Committee and in the congressional debates on passage of the amendment. That the courts will interpret the ERA responsibly and with an understanding of legislative intent is evident from the existing decisions interpreting equal rights amendments in those 16 States which have such amendments in their constitutions.

Based on this record, it is fair to say that:

ERA *will* enshrine in the Constitution the value judgment that sex discrimination is wrong.

ERA *will* require the Federal Government and each State to review and revise all laws and official practices to eliminate discrimination based on sex.

ERA *will* insure that governments do not enact future laws that discriminate on the basis of sex. Many State and Federal laws have been revised and new laws enacted to eliminate sex discrimination as a result of the debates on ERA. But these laws could be changed by new Congresses and new State legislatures, and failure to ratify the ERA may result in some losses of recent gains. A constitutional amendment provides a permanent basis for progress.

ERA *will* be the basis for recognition of the principle (ignored in most family law) that the homemaker's role in marriage has economic value and that marriage is a full partnership. Under Pennsylvania's ERA, for example, the State supreme court ruled in 1975 that nonmonetary contributions to a marriage, such as household work and child care, must be considered when a couple's household goods are divided as a result of divorce.

ERA *will* insure equality of opportunity in public schools, state colleges, and universities, employment training programs of Federal, State, or local governments, and in governmental recreation programs.

ERA *will* insure equal opportunity, privileges, and benefits in all aspects of Government employment.

ERA *will* insure that families of women workers receive the same benefits as families of men workers under the social security law, Government pension plans, and workers' compensation laws.

ERA *will* insure that married women can engage in business freely and dispose of separate or community property on the same basis as married men.

ERA will give the same rights to a woman as to a man in marital law and allow a married woman to maintain a separate domicile for voting purposes, for passports, for car registration, etc. (A husband may be in the military service and maintain his legal domicile "back home," but is wife may want to vote for the local school board where the kids go to school, for example.)

## WHAT ERA WILL NOT DO

ERA *will NOT* change or weaken family structure. Courts do not interfere in the private relationship of an ongoing marriage, and ERA will strengthen families by implicitly giving value to each spouse's contribution to and support of the other.

ERA *will NOT* require the States to permit homosexual marriage. The amendment is concerned with discrimination based on gender and has nothing to do with sexual behavior or relationships between people of the same sex. After the State of Washington had passed an Equal Rights Amendment to its own constitution, the State supreme court held that a State law prohibiting homosexual marriage was not invalidated.

ERA *will NOT* have any impact on abortion laws. The U.S. Supreme Court decisions on abortion were made under present constitutional provisions addressed to privacy issues and based on the 1st, 9th, and 14th Amendments.

ERA *will NOT* require co-ed bathrooms. The legislative history to which the courts would refer makes it clear that "the amendment would not require that dormitories or bathrooms be shared by men and women." Sexual equality will not be obtained at the expense of the constitutionally guaranteed right to privacy.

ERA *will NOT* require that there be as many women as men in combat roles in the military service, but it will give women equal access to the skills, training, education, and other benefits that military services provide. There is no draft now, but if a national emergency requires one in the future or if it is reinstated for any reason, women would be subject to the draft just as men would be, under a system that would undoubtedly provide for exemptions for specific categories, e.g., parents of dependent children, persons with physical, mental, or emotional illness, conscientious objectors, and others.

The military services would have the same right to assign women as they have to assign men, but this does not mean that women would be automatically assigned to combat, unless they volunteered for such duties. As a matter of fact, in modern warfare a very small percentage of men in the armed services actually serve in combat, and the decision as to who is best equipped for combat is up to the commanders. Meanwhile, to deny women the opportunity to freely enter the military services today is to deny them an equal expression of patriotism as well as career, educational, and job opportunities.

ERA *will NOT* be a "gigantic power grab by the Federal bureaucracy" to take over jurisdiction that now belongs to the States, as is frequently charged. Once ERA is ratified, States and the Federal Government have two years within which to bring their laws into conformity. If this is not done, the courts may declare invalid or extend to both sexes State or Federal laws or practices that are contrary to the ERA. The State will still be able to enact a new law or regulation that is in conformity. The first 10 amendments to the Constitution—the Bill of Rights—guarantee that the States will not pass laws infringing on freedom of speech, freedom of religion, freedom of the press, freedom from unreasonable search and seizure, the right to trial by jury, etc. None of these amendments denies States the right to enact laws in these areas, but they do not have the right to enact laws that violate these constitutional guarantees. Adoption of the ERA will guarantee that neither the States nor the Federal Government will pass laws or engage in official practices that discriminate because of gender.

ERA opponents cite, as the basis for some of their claims about the effects of the amendments, testimony by Professors of Law Paul Freund and Philip Kurland and interpretations of former Senator Sam

Ervin. However, they fail to quote these law professors on the importance of legislative history in interpreting the ERA. Both Freund and
Kurland testified in Congress before the committee reports on ERA
were issued and before the debates in the House and Senate that established the legislative history of the ERA and the intent of Congress in
approving the amendment.

Senator Ervin based his interpretation on his belief that the language of the amendment is so clear that the courts will have no choice
but to interpret it his way and that, therefore, they will not look to legislative history. However, all the other members of the Senate Judiciary
Committee and large majorities of both the House and Senate interpreted the language differently from Senator Ervin.

## WHERE IT STANDS NOW

The Equal Rights Amendment, the 27th Amendment, was passed by
a vote of 354 to 23 in the U.S. House of Representatives on October 12,
1971. The U.S. Senate approved it March 22, 1972 by a vote of 84 to 8
after decisively rejecting one by one, nine different proposals to alter
and defeat it. It will become part of the U.S Constitution when three-
fourths of the States (38) have ratified it, and it will go into effect two
years after the ratification date.

As of March 1978, ERA has been ratified by 35 States: Alaska,
California, Colorado, Connecticut, Delaware, Hawaii, Idaho, Indiana,
Iowa, Kansas, Kentucky, Maine, Maryland, Massachusetts, Michigan,
Minnesota, Montana, Nebraska, New Hampshire, New Jersey, New
Mexico, New York, North Dakota, Ohio, Oregon, Pennsylvania, Rhode
Island, South Dakota, Tennessee, Texas, Vermont, Washington, West
Virginia, Wisconsin, and Wyoming.

Three States—Idaho, Nebraska, and Tennessee—later voted to rescind ratification, a move of doubtful legality. An opinion issued by As-
sistant Attorney General John Harmon declares the States do not have
the power under the Constitution to rescind. Congressional precedents
and the 14th and 15th Amendments provide the underpinning for this
view.

Fifteen States have not ratified: Alabama, Arizona, Arkansas,

Florida, Georgia, Illinois, Louisiana, Mississippi, Missouri, Nevada, North Carolina, Oklahoma, South Carolina, Utah, and Virginia.

## WHO SUPPORTS ERA

ERA has been endorsed by the last six Presidents of the United States, passed by the Congress, ratified by 35 States, approved by the Democratic and Republican national committees, and supported by more than 200 organizations, including: American Association of University Women; American Baptist Women; American Bar Association; the AFL-CIO and 26 affiliated unions; American Home Economics Association; American Jewish Congress; American Veterans Committee; B'nai B'rith Women; Board of Church and Society; United Methodist Church; Catholic Women for the ERA; Child Welfare League of America; Christian Church (Disciples of Christ); Coalition of Labor Union Women; Common Cause; General Federation of Women's Clubs; Girl Scouts of the U.S.A.; League of Women Voters; Lutheran Church; NAACP; National Catholic Coalition for the ERA; National Coalition of American Nuns; National Council of Churches (of Christ); National Council of Jewish Women; National Council of Negro Women; National Federation of Business and Professional Women's Clubs; National Organization for Women; National Secretaries Association; National Woman's Party; National Women's Political Caucus; United Auto Workers; United Presbyterian Church, U.S.A.; and Young Women's Christian Association.

## THE OUTLOOK

Under a seven-year limitation set by Congress, ERA must be ratified by March 22, 1979. If it is not ratified by then, the amendment would have to be reintroduced in Congress and go through the entire ratification process again. However, in the opinion of the Department of Justice, Congress may vote to change the date by which ratification must be completed. A bill has been introduced by Congresswoman Elizabeth Holtzman to extend that deadline to 1986.

ERAmerica, a coalition of major organizations set up to fight for ratification, NOW, the League of Women Voters, the American Association of University Women, the Business and Professional Women, other groups and an overwhelming majority of the delegates to the National Women's Conference are making final ratification of ERA a priority.

The ratification battle has narrowed down to a few States where some legislators, despite public commitments to support ERA, have succumbed to last-minute political pressures and voted against it. Pro-ERA forces are conducting national education campaigns on the issue and are lobbying, fundraising, and organizing support and campaigning for defeat of anti-ERA legislators. More than 80 major national organizations are boycotting nonratified States and are cancelling meetings that were scheduled to be held there. An important factor in the National Commission's decision to hold its National Women's Conference in Houston was that Texas has ratified the ERA.

Women have waited more than 200 years for the equality promised by the Declaration of Independence to all men. Two years after the United States of America celebrated its Bicentennial, it is time to extend democracy to all American citizens and to put women into the Constitution at last.

# Convention on the Elimination of All Forms of Discrimination Against Women (CEDAW)

*CEDAW was adopted on December 18, 1979, by the United Nations General Assembly, and entered into force as an international treaty on September 3, 1981 after the twentieth country had ratified it. Signed by President Jimmy Carter in 1980, it was never ratified by the Senate (two-thirds vote required for ratification). To date, 187 other countries have ratified CEDAW, all countries in the world but the United States, Iran, Somalia, Sudan, South Sudan, and two small Pacific Island nations—Palau and Tonga.*

### *The States Parties to the present Convention,*

Noting that the Charter of the United Nations reaffirms faith in fundamental human rights, in the dignity and worth of the human person and in the equal rights of men and women,

Noting that the Universal Declaration of Human Rights affirms the principle of the inadmissibility of discrimination and proclaims that all human beings are born free and equal in dignity and rights and that everyone is entitled to all the rights and freedoms set forth therein, without distinction of any kind, including distinction based on sex,

Noting that the States Parties to the International Covenants on Human Rights have the obligation to ensure the equal rights of men and women to enjoy all economic, social, cultural, civil and political rights,

Considering the international conventions concluded under the auspices of the United Nations and the specialized agencies promoting equality of rights of men and women,

Noting also the resolutions, declarations and recommendations adopted by the United Nations and the specialized agencies promoting equality of rights of men and women,

Concerned, however, that despite these various instruments extensive discrimination against women continues to exist,

Recalling that discrimination against women violates the principles of equality of rights and respect for human dignity, is an obstacle to the participation of women, on equal terms with men, in the political, social, economic and cultural life of their countries, hampers the growth of the prosperity of society and the family and makes more difficult the full development of the potentialities of women in the service of their countries and of humanity,

Concerned that in situations of poverty women have the least access to food, health, education, training and opportunities for employment and other needs,

Convinced that the establishment of the new international economic order based on equity and justice will contribute significantly towards the promotion of equality between men and women,

Emphasizing that the eradication of apartheid, all forms of racism, racial discrimination, colonialism, neo-colonialism, aggression, foreign occupation and domination and interference in the internal affairs of States is essential to the full enjoyment of the rights of men and women,

Affirming that the strengthening of international peace and security, the relaxation of international tension, mutual co-operation among all States irrespective of their social and economic systems, general and complete disarmament, in particular nuclear disarmament under strict and effective international control, the affirmation of the principles of justice, equality and mutual benefit in relations among countries and the realization of the right of peoples under alien and colonial domination and foreign occupation to self-determination and independence, as well as respect for national sovereignty and territorial integrity, will promote social progress and development and as a consequence will contribute to the attainment of full equality between men and women,

Convinced that the full and complete development of a country, the welfare of the world and the cause of peace require the maximum participation of women on equal terms with men in all fields,

Bearing in mind the great contribution of women to the welfare of the family and to the development of society, so far not fully recognized, the social significance of maternity and the role of both parents in the family and in the upbringing of children, and aware that the role of women in procreation should not be a basis for discrimination but that the upbringing of children requires a sharing of responsibility between men and women and society as a whole,

Aware that a change in the traditional role of men as well as the role of women in society and in the family is needed to achieve full equality between men and women,

Determined to implement the principles set forth in the Declaration on the Elimination of Discrimination against Women and, for that purpose, to adopt the measures required for the elimination of such discrimination in all its forms and manifestations,

Have agreed on the following:

## PART I

### Article I

For the purposes of the present Convention, the term "discrimination against women" shall mean any distinction, exclusion or restriction made on the basis of sex which has the effect or purpose of impairing or nullifying the recognition, enjoyment or exercise by women, irrespective of their marital status, on a basis of equality of men and women, of human rights and fundamental freedoms in the political, economic, social, cultural, civil or any other field.

## Article 2

States Parties condemn discrimination against women in all its forms, agree to pursue by all appropriate means and without delay a policy of eliminating discrimination against women and, to this end, undertake:

(a) To embody the principle of the equality of men and women in their national constitutions or other appropriate legislation if not yet incorporated therein and to ensure, through law and other appropriate means, the practical realization of this principle;

(b) To adopt appropriate legislative and other measures, including sanctions where appropriate, prohibiting all discrimination against women;

(c) To establish legal protection of the rights of women on an equal basis with men and to ensure through competent national tribunals and other public institutions the effective protection of women against any act of discrimination;

(d) To refrain from engaging in any act or practice of discrimination against women and to ensure that public authorities and institutions shall act in conformity with this obligation;

(e) To take all appropriate measures to eliminate discrimination against women by any person, organization or enterprise;

(f) To take all appropriate measures, including legislation, to modify or abolish existing laws, regulations, customs and practices which constitute discrimination against women;

(g) To repeal all national penal provisions which constitute discrimination against women.

## Article 3

States Parties shall take in all fields, in particular in the political, social, economic and cultural fields, all appropriate measures, including legislation, to ensure the full development and advancement of women, for the purpose of guaranteeing them the exercise and enjoyment of human rights and fundamental freedoms on a basis of equality with men.

## Article 4

1. Adoption by States Parties of temporary special measures aimed at accelerating de facto equality between men and women shall not be considered discrimination as defined in the present Convention, but shall in no way entail as a consequence the maintenance of unequal or separate standards; these measures shall be discontinued when the objectives of equality of opportunity and treatment have been achieved.

2. Adoption by States Parties of special measures, including those measures contained in the present Convention, aimed at protecting maternity shall not be considered discriminatory.

## Article 5

States Parties shall take all appropriate measures:

(a) To modify the social and cultural patterns of conduct of men and women, with a view to achieving the elimination of prejudices and customary and all other practices which are based on the idea of the inferiority or the superiority of either of the sexes or on stereotyped roles for men and women;

(b) To ensure that family education includes a proper understanding of maternity as a social function and the recognition of the common responsibility of men and women in the upbringing and development of their children, it being understood that the interest of the children is the primordial consideration in all cases.

## Article 6

States Parties shall take all appropriate measures, including legislation, to suppress all forms of traffic in women and exploitation of prostitution of women.

## PART II

## Article 7

States Parties shall take all appropriate measures to eliminate discrimination against women in the political and public life of the country and, in particular, shall ensure to women, on equal terms with men, the right:

(a) To vote in all elections and public referenda and to be eligible for election to all publicly elected bodies;

(b) To participate in the formulation of government policy and the implementation thereof and to hold public office and perform all public functions at all levels of government;

(c) To participate in non-governmental organizations and associations concerned with the public and political life of the country.

## Article 8

States Parties shall take all appropriate measures to ensure to women, on equal terms with men and without any discrimination, the opportunity to represent their Governments at the international level and to participate in the work of international organizations.

## Article 9

1. States Parties shall grant women equal rights with men to acquire, change or retain their nationality. They shall ensure in particular that neither marriage to an alien nor change of nationality by the husband during marriage shall automatically change the nationality of the wife, render her stateless or force upon her the nationality of the husband.

2. States Parties shall grant women equal rights with men with respect to the nationality of their children.

## PART III

### Article 10

States Parties shall take all appropriate measures to eliminate discrimination against women in order to ensure to them equal rights with men in the field of education and in particular to ensure, on a basis of equality of men and women:

(a) The same conditions for career and vocational guidance, for access to studies and for the achievement of diplomas in educational establishments of all categories in rural as well as in urban areas; this equality shall be ensured in pre-school, general, technical, professional and higher technical education, as well as in all types of vocational training;

(b) Access to the same curricula, the same examinations, teaching staff with qualifications of the same standard and school premises and equipment of the same quality;

(c) The elimination of any stereotyped concept of the roles of men and women at all levels and in all forms of education by encouraging coeducation and other types of education which will help to achieve this aim and, in particular, by the revision of textbooks and school programmes and the adaptation of teaching methods;

(d) The same opportunities to benefit from scholarships and other study grants;

(e) The same opportunities for access to programmes of continuing education, including adult and functional literacy programmes, particularly those aimed at reducing, at the earliest possible time, any gap in education existing between men and women;

(f) The reduction of female student drop-out rates and the organization of programmes for girls and women who have left school prematurely;

(g) The same opportunities to participate actively in sports and physical education;

(h) Access to specific educational information to help to ensure the health and well-being of families, including information and advice on family planning.

## *Article 11*

1. States Parties shall take all appropriate measures to eliminate discrimination against women in the field of employment in order to ensure, on a basis of equality of men and women, the same rights, in particular:

(a) The right to work as an inalienable right of all human beings;

(b) The right to the same employment opportunities, including the application of the same criteria for selection in matters of employment;

(c) The right to free choice of profession and employment, the right to promotion, job security and all benefits and conditions of service and the right to receive vocational training and retraining, including apprenticeships, advanced vocational training and recurrent training;

(d) The right to equal remuneration, including benefits, and to equal treatment in respect of work of equal value, as well as equality of treatment in the evaluation of the quality of work;

(e) The right to social security, particularly in cases of retirement, unemployment, sickness, invalidity and old age and other incapacity to work, as well as the right to paid leave;

(f) The right to protection of health and to safety in working conditions, including the safeguarding of the function of reproduction.

2. In order to prevent discrimination against women on the grounds of marriage or maternity and to ensure their effective right to work, States Parties shall take appropriate measures:

(a) To prohibit, subject to the imposition of sanctions, dismissal on the grounds of pregnancy or of maternity leave and discrimination in dismissals on the basis of marital status;

(b) To introduce maternity leave with pay or with comparable social benefits without loss of former employment, seniority or social allowances;

(c) To encourage the provision of the necessary supporting social services to enable parents to combine family obligations with work responsibilities and participation in public life, in particular through promoting the establishment and development of a network of childcare facilities;

(d) To provide special protection to women during pregnancy in types of work proved to be harmful to them.

3. Protective legislation relating to matters covered in this article shall be reviewed periodically in the light of scientific and technological knowledge and shall be revised, repealed or extended as necessary.

### Article 12

1. States Parties shall take all appropriate measures to eliminate discrimination against women in the field of health care in order to ensure, on a basis of equality of men and women, access to health care services, including those related to family planning.

2. Notwithstanding the provisions of paragraph 1 of this article, States Parties shall ensure to women appropriate services in connection with pregnancy, confinement and the post-natal period, granting free services where necessary, as well as adequate nutrition during pregnancy and lactation.

### Article 13

States Parties shall take all appropriate measures to eliminate discrimination against women in other areas of economic and social life in order to ensure, on a basis of equality of men and women, the same rights, in particular:

(a) The right to family benefits;

(b) The right to bank loans, mortgages and other forms of financial credit;

(c) The right to participate in recreational activities, sports and all aspects of cultural life.

## Article 14

1. States Parties shall take into account the particular problems faced by rural women and the significant roles which rural women play in the economic survival of their families, including their work in the non-monetized sectors of the economy, and shall take all appropriate measures to ensure the application of the provisions of the present Convention to women in rural areas.

2. States Parties shall take all appropriate measures to eliminate discrimination against women in rural areas in order to ensure, on a basis of equality of men and women, that they participate in and benefit from rural development and, in particular, shall ensure to such women the right:

(a) To participate in the elaboration and implementation of development planning at all levels;

(b) To have access to adequate health care facilities, including information, counselling and services in family planning;

(c) To benefit directly from social security programmes;

(d) To obtain all types of training and education, formal and non-formal, including that relating to functional literacy, as well as, inter alia, the benefit of all community and extension services, in order to increase their technical proficiency;

(e) To organize self-help groups and co-operatives in order to obtain equal access to economic opportunities through employment or self-employment;

(f) To participate in all community activities;

(g) To have access to agricultural credit and loans, marketing facilities, appropriate technology and equal treatment in land and agrarian reform as well as in land resettlement schemes;

(h) To enjoy adequate living conditions, particularly in relation to housing, sanitation, electricity and water supply, transport and communications.

## PART IV

### Article 15

1. States Parties shall accord to women equality with men before the law.

2. States Parties shall accord to women, in civil matters, a legal capacity identical to that of men and the same opportunities to exercise that capacity. In particular, they shall give women equal rights to conclude contracts and to administer property and shall treat them equally in all stages of procedure in courts and tribunals.

3. States Parties agree that all contracts and all other private instruments of any kind with a legal effect which is directed at restricting the legal capacity of women shall be deemed null and void.

4. States Parties shall accord to men and women the same rights with regard to the law relating to the movement of persons and the freedom to choose their residence and domicile.

### Article 16

1. States Parties shall take all appropriate measures to eliminate discrimination against women in all matters relating to marriage and

family relations and in particular shall ensure, on a basis of equality of men and women:

(a) The same right to enter into marriage;

(b) The same right freely to choose a spouse and to enter into marriage only with their free and full consent;

(c) The same rights and responsibilities during marriage and at its dissolution;

(d) The same rights and responsibilities as parents, irrespective of their marital status, in matters relating to their children; in all cases the interests of the children shall be paramount;

(e) The same rights to decide freely and responsibly on the number and spacing of their children and to have access to the information, education and means to enable them to exercise these rights;

(f) The same rights and responsibilities with regard to guardianship, wardship, trusteeship and adoption of children, or similar institutions where these concepts exist in national legislation; in all cases the interests of the children shall be paramount;

(g) The same personal rights as husband and wife, including the right to choose a family name, a profession and an occupation;

(h) The same rights for both spouses in respect of the ownership, acquisition, management, administration, enjoyment and disposition of property, whether free of charge or for a valuable consideration.

2. The betrothal and the marriage of a child shall have no legal effect, and all necessary action, including legislation, shall be taken to specify a minimum age for marriage and to make the registration of marriages in an official registry compulsory.

**PART V**

*Article 17*

1. For the purpose of considering the progress made in the implementation of the present Convention, there shall be established a Committee on the Elimination of Discrimination against Women (hereinafter referred to as the Committee) consisting, at the time of entry into force of the Convention, of eighteen and, after ratification of or accession to the Convention by the thirty-fifth State Party, of twenty-three experts of high moral standing and competence in the field covered by the Convention. The experts shall be elected by States Parties from among their nationals and shall serve in their personal capacity, consideration being given to equitable geographical distribution and to the representation of the different forms of civilization as well as the principal legal systems.

2. The members of the Committee shall be elected by secret ballot from a list of persons nominated by States Parties. Each State Party may nominate one person from among its own nationals.

3. The initial election shall be held six months after the date of the entry into force of the present Convention. At least three months before the date of each election the Secretary-General of the United Nations shall address a letter to the States Parties inviting them to submit their nominations within two months. The Secretary-General shall prepare a list in alphabetical order of all persons thus nominated, indicating the States Parties which have nominated them, and shall submit it to the States Parties.

4. Elections of the members of the Committee shall be held at a meeting of States Parties convened by the Secretary-General at United Nations Headquarters. At that meeting, for which two thirds of the States Parties shall constitute a quorum, the persons elected to the Committee shall be those nominees who obtain the largest number of votes and an absolute majority of the votes of the representatives of States Parties present and voting.

5. The members of the Committee shall be elected for a term of four years. However, the terms of nine of the members elected at the first election shall expire at the end of two years; immediately after the first election the names of these nine members shall be chosen by lot by the Chairman of the Committee.

6. The election of the five additional members of the Committee shall be held in accordance with the provisions of paragraphs 2, 3 and 4 of this article, following the thirty-fifth ratification or accession. The terms of two of the additional members elected on this occasion shall expire at the end of two years, the names of these two members having been chosen by lot by the Chairman of the Committee.

7. For the filling of casual vacancies, the State Party whose expert has ceased to function as a member of the Committee shall appoint another expert from among its nationals, subject to the approval of the Committee.

8. The members of the Committee shall, with the approval of the General Assembly, receive emoluments from United Nations resources on such terms and conditions as the Assembly may decide, having regard to the importance of the Committee's responsibilities.

9. The Secretary-General of the United Nations shall provide the necessary staff and facilities for the effective performance of the functions of the Committee under the present Convention.

## Article 18

1. States Parties undertake to submit to the Secretary-General of the United Nations, for consideration by the Committee, a report on the legislative, judicial, administrative or other measures which they have adopted to give effect to the provisions of the present Convention and on the progress made in this respect:

(a) Within one year after the entry into force for the State concerned;

(b) Thereafter at least every four years and further whenever the Committee so requests.

2. Reports may indicate factors and difficulties affecting the degree of fulfilment of obligations under the present Convention.

## Article 19

1. The Committee shall adopt its own rules of procedure.

2. The Committee shall elect its officers for a term of two years.

## Article 20

1. The Committee shall normally meet for a period of not more than two weeks annually in order to consider the reports submitted in accordance with article 18 of the present Convention.

2. The meetings of the Committee shall normally be held at United Nations Headquarters or at any other convenient place as determined by the Committee.

## Article 21

1. The Committee shall, through the Economic and Social Council, report annually to the General Assembly of the United Nations on its activities and may make suggestions and general recommendations based on the examination of reports and information received from the States Parties. Such suggestions and general recommendations shall be included in the report of the Committee together with comments, if any, from States Parties.

2. The Secretary-General of the United Nations shall transmit the reports of the Committee to the Commission on the Status of Women for its information.

## Article 22

The specialized agencies shall be entitled to be represented at the consideration of the implementation of such provisions of the present

Convention as fall within the scope of their activities. The Committee may invite the specialized agencies to submit reports on the implementation of the Convention in areas falling within the scope of their activities.

## PART VI

### *Article 23*

Nothing in the present Convention shall affect any provisions that are more conducive to the achievement of equality between men and women which may be contained:

(a) In the legislation of a State Party; or

(b) In any other international convention, treaty or agreement in force for that State.

### *Article 24*

States Parties undertake to adopt all necessary measures at the national level aimed at achieving the full realization of the rights recognized in the present Convention.

### *Article 25*

1. The present Convention shall be open for signature by all States.

2. The Secretary-General of the United Nations is designated as the depositary of the present Convention.

3. The present Convention is subject to ratification. Instruments of ratification shall be deposited with the Secretary-General of the United Nations.

4. The present Convention shall be open to accession by all States. Accession shall be effected by the deposit of an instrument of accession with the Secretary-General of the United Nations.

## Article 26

1. A request for the revision of the present Convention may be made at any time by any State Party by means of a notification in writing addressed to the Secretary-General of the United Nations.

2. The General Assembly of the United Nations shall decide upon the steps, if any, to be taken in respect of such a request.

## Article 27

1. The present Convention shall enter into force on the thirtieth day after the date of deposit with the Secretary-General of the United Nations of the twentieth instrument of ratification or accession.

2. For each State ratifying the present Convention or acceding to it after the deposit of the twentieth instrument of ratification or accession, the Convention shall enter into force on the thirtieth day after the date of the deposit of its own instrument of ratification or accession.

## Article 28

1. The Secretary-General of the United Nations shall receive and circulate to all States the text of reservations made by States at the time of ratification or accession.

2. A reservation incompatible with the object and purpose of the present Convention shall not be permitted.

3. Reservations may be withdrawn at any time by notification to this effect addressed to the Secretary-General of the United Nations, who shall then inform all States thereof. Such notification shall take effect on the date on which it is received.

## Article 29

1. Any dispute between two or more States Parties concerning the interpretation or application of the present Convention which is not

settled by negotiation shall, at the request of one of them, be submitted to arbitration. If within six months from the date of the request for arbitration the parties are unable to agree on the organization of the arbitration, any one of those parties may refer the dispute to the International Court of Justice by request in conformity with the Statute of the Court.

2. Each State Party may at the time of signature or ratification of the present Convention or accession thereto declare that it does not consider itself bound by paragraph 1 of this article. The other States Parties shall not be bound by that paragraph with respect to any State Party which has made such a reservation.

3. Any State Party which has made a reservation in accordance with paragraph 2 of this article may at any time withdraw that reservation by notification to the Secretary-General of the United Nations.

## Article 30

The present Convention, the Arabic, Chinese, English, French, Russian and Spanish texts of which are equally authentic, shall be deposited with the Secretary-General of the United Nations.

IN WITNESS WHEREOF the undersigned, duly authorized, have signed the present Convention.

# NOTES

## INTRODUCTION BY GLORIA STEINEM

1. Abigail Adams, letter to John Adams, March 31, 1776, Braintree, Massachusetts, reprinted as "All Men Would Be Tyrants If They Could," *Lapham's Quarterly*, Spring 2014, www.laphamsquarterly.org/voices-in-time/all-men-would-be-tyrants-if-they-could.php?page=all.

2. Thomas Jefferson, letter to Samuel Kercheval, September 5, 1816, in *The Writings of Thomas Jefferson*, ed. Paul L. Ford (New York: G.P. Putnam's Sons, 1899): 10:45–46, fn1.

3. Gunnar Myrdal, *An American Dilemma: The Negro Problem and Modern Democracy* (New York: Harper & Brothers, 1944), 1078.

## INTRODUCTION

1. Calvin Massey, "The Originalist: Justice Antonin Scalia," *California Lawyer*, January 2011, www.callawyer.com/Clstory.cfm?eid=913358.

2. "Justice Ginsburg on Women as Judges," Thomas Jefferson School of Law, San Diego, February 8, 2013, C-SPAN broadcast, www.c-span.org/video/?310892–1/justice-ginsburg-women-judges.

3. For more information on Alice Paul, see the Alice Paul Institute website at www.alicepaul.org.

4. For more information, see the Equal Rights Amendment website, www.equalrightsamendment.org.

5. Alaska, California, Colorado, Delaware, Hawaii, Idaho, Iowa, Kansas, Kentucky, Maryland, Massachusetts, Michigan, New Hampshire, Nebraska, New Jersey, New York, Pennsylvania, Rhode Island, Texas, Tennessee, West Virginia, and Wisconsin.

6. Connecticut, Minnesota, New Mexico, Oregon, South Dakota, Vermont, Washington, and Wyoming.

7. Maine, Montana, and Ohio in 1974 and North Dakota in 1975.

8. Indiana.

9. Nebraska voted to rescind ratification in 1973, Tennessee in 1974, Idaho in 1977, and Kentucky in 1978. South Dakota voted in 1979 to limit the validity of its ratification to the expiration of the seven-year deadline that year.

10. For a complete history of the ERA, see Mary Frances Berry, *Why ERA Failed:*

*Politics, Women's Rights, and the Amending Process of the Constitution* (Bloomington: Indiana University Press, 1988).

11. The validity of votes to rescind ratification is an open question, which is discussed in the last chapter of this book.

12. A Gallup poll in 1981 found that 63 percent of Americans polled supported the ERA, and a Harris poll in 1982 found that 73 percent of Americans supported the ERA. State polling results produced comparable numbers. See feminism101.com/timelineera.html.

13. Eleanor Smeal, in discussion with the author, May 23, 2014.

14. Berry, *Why ERA Failed*, 81.

15. Jennifer E. Manning and Ida A. Brudnick, *Women in the United States Congress, 1917–2014: Biographical and Committee Assignment Information, and Listings by State and Congress* (Washington, DC: Congressional Research Service, 2014).

16. See Abby Ferla, "ERA: Historical Curiosity or Needed Weapon Against Bias?," Remapping Debate, www.remappingdebate.org/article/era-historical-curiosity-or -needed-weapon-against-bias-today?page=0,3.

17. Kalli Joy Gray, "Daily Kos/Service Employees International Union Poll: Huge Majority of Americans Support Equal Rights for Women in Constitution," *Daily Kos*, April 24, 2012, www.dailykos.com/story/2012/04/24/1086021/-Daily-Kos-SEIU-poll -Huge-majority-of-Americans-support-equal-rights-for-women-in-Constitution#.

18. Laura Turquet, *2011–2012 Progress of the World's Women: In Pursuit of Justice* (New York: UN Women, 2011), progress.unwomen.org/pdfs/EN-Report-Progress.pdf.

19. Eleanor Roosevelt, "In Your Hands," speech delivered on the tenth anniversary of the Universal Declaration of Human Rights, March 27, 1958.

## PAY INEQUITY

1. Monee Fields-White, "She's Taking on Walmart," *The Root*, June 24, 2010, www.theroot.com/articles/culture/2010/06/interview_betty_dukes_on_the_walmart _genderbias_lawsuit.html; "Supreme Court Weighs Massive Lawsuit Accusing Retail Giant Wal-Mart for Sexual Discrimination Against Female Workers," *Democracy Now!* March 11, 2011, www.democracynow.org/2011/3/31/supreme_court_hears_weighs _massive_suit.

2. See the WAGE Project, www.wageproject.org/files/costs.php.

3. See ibid.

4. Title VII of the Civil Rights Act of 1964, §703(a)(1) and (2), 42 U.S.C. § 2000e-2(a) (2000).

5. Associated Press, "Talks to Settle Women's Pay Suit," June 6, 1984.

6. Kouba v. Allstate Insurance Company, 521 F. Supp. 148 (1981).

7. Kouba v. Allstate Insurance Company, 691 F.2d 873 (Ninth Cir. 1982). The case was remanded for further consideration of the legitimate business reasons set forth to justify the use of prior salary, and eventually the case was settled.

8. "Payments to Women by Allstate," *New York Times*, October 2, 1984.

9. Griggs v. Duke Power Co., 401 U.S. 424, 432 (1971).

10. Title VII, §703(k)(1)(i), 42 U.S.C. § 2000e-2(k) (2000).

11. Washington v. Davis, 426 U.S. 229, 243 (1976).

12. Ibid. at 238–39.

13. Ward's Cove Packing v. Antonio, 490 U.S. 656 (1989).

14. Ibid. at 678.

15. Ibid. at 678, n.2.

16. Civil Rights Act of 1991 (Pub. L. No. 102–166) codified as amended throughout 42 U.S.C.

17. Dukes v. Wal-Mart Stores, Inc., 222 F.R.D. 137 (N.D. Cal. 2004).

18. Dukes v. Wal-Mart Stores, Inc., 603 F.3d. 571 (Ninth Cir. 2000) (en banc).

19. Wal-Mart Stores, Inc., v. Dukes et al., 113 S. Ct. 2541 (2011).

20. Following the decision, women had to bring their sex discrimination claims against Walmart store by store, making their quest for justice much more difficult.

21. Fields-White, "She's Taking on Walmart."

22. "Supreme Court Weighs Massive Lawsuit."

23. *Wal-Mart Stores, Inc.*, 113 S. Ct. at 2545.

24. Ibid. at 2562 (Ginsburg, J., dissenting).

25. Ledbetter v. Goodyear Tire and Rubber Co., 421 F.3d 1196 (Eleventh Cir. 2005).

26. United Airlines, Inc. v. Evans, 431 U.S. 553, 558 (1977).

27. *Separate and Not Equal? Gender Segregation in the Labor Market and the Gender Wage Gap*, Institute for Women's Policy Research Briefing Paper, September 2010.

28. Brad Plumer, "Five Shocking Facts about Child Care in the United States," *Washington Post*, April 15, 2013.

29. County of Washington v. Gunther, 452 U.S. 161, 180 (1981).

30. Christensen v. State of Iowa, 563 F.2d 353, 356 (C.A. Iowa, 1977).

31. American Federation of State, County, and Municipal Employees v. State of Washington, 578 F. Supp. 846, 865–71 (W.D. Wash. 1983).

32. American Federation of State, County, and Municipal Employees v. State of Washington, 770 F.2d 1401, 1406 (Ninth Cir. 1985).

33. Ibid.

34. Lemons v. City of Denver, 620 F.2d 228, 229 (Tenth Cir. 1980).

35. *Lemons*, 1978 WL 13938, at *3 (D.Colo. Apr. 28, 1978).

36. Directive 76/117/EEC of the Council of European Communities of 10 February 1975 on the Approximation of the Laws of Member States Relating to the Application of the Principle of Equal Pay for Men and Women.

37. See Catharine A. MacKinnon, *Sex Equality*, 2nd ed. (New York: Foundation Press, 2007), 177–96.

38. Rexroat v. Arizona Department of Education, 2013 WL 85222, at *6 (D. Ariz. Jan. 7, 2013), quoting *Kouba* at 876–77.

39. Paycheck Fairness Act, S. 2199 (2014) (previously introduced as S.84 on January 23, 2013, with H.R. 377, introduced in the House of Representatives on that same date).

## PREGNANCY DISCRIMINATION

1. Yuki Noguchi, "When Being Pregnant Also Means Being Out of a Job," *All Things Considered*, National Public Radio, April 17, 2014, www.npr.org/2014/04/17/304070037/when-being-pregnant-also-means-being-out-of-a-job.

2. Carol Kleiman, "Court Victory in War on Sex Bias Was Not Without Serious Casualties," *Chicago Tribune*, June 22, 1987.

3. Pat Morrison, "Job Litigant Asked God to Guide Justices," *Los Angeles Times*, January 14, 1987, articles.latimes.com/1987–01–14/news/mn-3375_1_custody.

4. "Fair Treatment for Pregnant Workers: Natasha Jackson's Story," National Women's Law Center and A Better Balance, June 18, 2013, www.nwlc.org/resource/fair-treatment-pregnant-workers-natasha-jacksons-story.

5. Jennifer Ludden, "Pushed Off the Job While Pregnant," *All Things Considered*, National Public Radio, June 11, 2013, www.npr.org/2013/06/11/189207542/pushed-off-the-job-while-pregnant.

6. Clark v. California Employment Stabilization Commission, 166 Cal.App.2d 326, 332 (Dist. Ct. App. Cal. 1958).

7. Rentzer v. Unemployment Appeals Board, 32 Cal.App.3d 605, 604–607 (Dist. Ct. App. Cal. 1958).

8. "Estimated Pregnancy Rates and Rates of Pregnancy Outcomes for the United States, 1990–2008," National Vital Statistics Report, June 20, 2012, www.cdc.gov/nchs/data/nvsr/nvsr60/nvsr60_07.pdf.

9. Fred Strebeigh, *Equal: Women Reshape American Law* (New York: W.W. Norton, 2009), 91.

10. Aiello v. Hansen, 359 F. Supp. 792, 801 (N.D. Cal. 1973).

11. Geduldig v. Aiello, 417 U.S. 484, 496 (1974).

12. Ibid. at 496, 497.

13. Ibid. at 500, 501.

14. Gilbert v. General Electric Company, 375 F. Supp. 367 (1974).

15. General Electric Co. v. Gilbert, 429 U.S. 125, 149 (1976).

16. Ibid. at 153.

17. Title VII, 42 U.S.C. § 2000e(b) (2000).

18. California Government Code §12945(b)(2) (West 2005).

19. California Federal Savings & Loan Assoc. v. Guerra, F., 479 U.S. 272, 280 (1987).

20. California Federal Savings and Loan Association v. Guerra F., 758 F.2d 390, 391 (Ninth Cir. 1985).

21. Ibid. at 396.

22. *California Federal Savings and Loan Assoc.*, 479 U.S. at 273.

23. Ibid. at 286.

24. *General Electric Co.*, 429 U.S. citing 124 Cong Rec. 21442 and 36818 (1978).

25. *California Federal Savings and Loan Assoc.*, 479 U.S. at 290.

26. Kleiman, "Court Victory in War on Sex Bias."

27. Newport News Shipbuilding and Dry Dock Co. v. EEOC, 667 F.2d 448 (Fourth Cir. 1982).

28. EEOC v. Lockheed Missiles & Space Co., 680 F.2d 1243 (Ninth Cir. 1982).

29. Newport News Shipbuilding and Dry Dock Co. v. EEOC, 462 U.S. 669 (1983).

30. Title VII, 42 U.S.C. § 2000e(b).

31. Young v. United Parcel Service, Inc., 707 F.3d 437, 448 (Fourth Cir. 2013).

32. Urbano v. Continental Airlines, Inc., 138 F.3d 204 (Fifth Cir. 1998); Reeves v. Swift Transportation Company, Inc., 446 F.3d 637 (Sixth Cir. 2006); Serednyj v. Beverly Healthcare, LLC, 656 F.3d 540 (Seventh Cir. 2011).

33. "It Shouldn't Be a Heavy Lift: Fair Treatment for Pregnant Workers," National Women's Law Center and A Better Balance, June 18, 2013; Peggy Young's story, 15, available at www.abetterbalance.org/web/images/stories/ItShouldntBeAHeavyLift .pdf.

34. Ibid., Svetlana Arizanovska's story, 18; Arizanovska v. Wal-Mart Stores, Inc., 682 F.3d 698 (Seventh Cir. 2012).

35. "It Shouldn't Be a Heavy Lift," Doris Garcia's story (under the pseudonym Guadalupe Hernandez), 4, www.nwlc.org/resource/fair-treatment-pregnant-workers-guada lupe-hernandezs-story.

36. Complaint filed on February 24, 2014, in the U.S. District Court for the District of Columbia, Doris Nohemi Garcia Hernandez v. Chipotle Mexican Grill, Inc., available at s3.documentcloud.org/documents/1028683/chipotle-lawsuit.pdf.

37. Burwell v. Hobby Lobby Stores, Inc., 134 S. Ct. 2751 (2014).

38. Ibid.

39. Wheaton College v. Burwell, 134 S. Ct. 2806 (2014).

40. Ibid.

## VIOLENCE AGAINST WOMEN

1. See ACLU, "Domestic Violence & Human Rights: Lenahan v. USA," www.aclu .org/womens-rights/domestic-violence-human-rights-lenahan-v-usa.

2. Fred Strebeigh, *Equal: Women Reshape American Law* (New York: W.W. Norton, 2009), 426.

3. Brzonkala v. Virginia Polytechnic Institute and State University, 169 F.3d 820 (Fourth Cir. 1999).

4. "Domestic Violence: Not Just a Family Matter," Hearing Before the Subcommittee on Crime and Criminal Justice of the House Committee on the Judiciary, 103d Cong., H.R. Conf. Rep. No. 103–711 (1994), 385.

5. Violence Against Women Act of 1994, 42 U.S.C. § 13981.

6. Strebeigh, *Equal*, 344.

7. Ibid., 351.

8. Ibid., 344.

9. See Liu v. Striuli, 36 F. Supp.2d 452 (D.R.I. 1999); Ziegler v. Ziegler, 28 F. Supp.2d 601 (E.D. Wash. 1998); Crisonino v. New York City Housing Authority, 985 F. Supp. 385 (S.D.N.Y. 1997); Anisimov v. Lake, 982 F. Supp. 531 (N.D. Ill. 1997); Seaton v. Seaton, 971 F. Supp. 1188 (E.D. Tenn. 1997); Doe v. Hartz, 970 F. Supp. 1375 (N.D. Iowa 1997), rev'd on other grounds, 134 F.3d 1339 (Eighth Cir. 1998); Doe v. Doe, 929 F. Supp. 608 (D. Conn. 1996); Timm v. DeLong, 59 F. Supp. 2d 944 (D. Neb. 1998); Mattison v. Click Corp. of America, Inc., 1998 WL 32597 (E.D. Pa. Jan. 27, 1998).

10. Brzonkala v. Virginia Polytechnic Institute and State University, 132 F.3d 949 (Fourth Cir. 1997) (three-member panel).

11. *Brzonkala*, 169 F.3d 820.

12. United States v. Harris, 106 U.S. 629 (1883).

13. "An Act to protect all citizens in their civil and legal rights." Civil Rights Act of 1875, 18 Stat. Part III, p. 335.

14. Civil Rights Cases, 109 U.S. 3 (1883).

15. Ibid. at 24.

16. Bradwell v. Illinois, 83 U.S. 130, 141 (1872).

17. *Civil Rights Cases*, 109 U.S. at 24 (1883).

18. Ibid. at 61 (Harlan, J., dissenting).

19. Ibid.

20. Ibid. at 54 (Harlan, J., dissenting).

21. S.Rep. No. 103-138 (1993), 54.

22. H.R. Rep. No. 103-395 (1993), 26; S.Rep. No. 103-138 (1993), 37.

23. Women and Violence: Hearing Before the Committee on the Judiciary, 101st Cong. 58 (1990) (statement of Helen K. Neuborne); S. Rep. No. 103-138, at 41.

24. *Brzonkala*, 169 F.3d at 826.

25. United States v. Alfonso Lopez, Jr., 514 U.S. 549, 567 (1995).

26. United States. v. Morrison, 529 U.S. 598, 613 (2000).

27. Ibid. at 620.

28. Ibid. at 621, citing Shelley v. Kraemer, 334 U.S. 1, 13, and n. 12 (1948).

29. *Congressional Globe*, 42d Cong., 1st sess., App. 153 (1871) (statement of Rep. Garfield).

30. *Morrison*, 529 U.S. at 622.

31. Ibid. at 624.

32. Ibid. at 661 citing *Crimes of Violence Motivated by Gender*, Hearing Before the

Subcommittee on Civil and Constitutional Rights of the House Committee on the Judiciary, 103d Cong., 1st sess., 34–36 (1993).

33. Castle Rock v. Gonzales, 545 U.S. 748, 753 (2005).

34. DeShaney v. Winnebago County Department of Social Services, 489 U.S. 189, 195 (1989).

35. Gonzales v. City of Castle Rock, 307 F.3d 1258, 1265 (Tenth Cir. 2002).

36. *Castle Rock*, 545 U.S. at 759.

37. Ibid. at 760 (citing ABA Standards for Criminal Justice).

38. Ibid. at 760, citing Gonzales v. City of Castle Rock, 366 F.3d 1093, 1109 (Tenth Cir. 2004).

39. Ibid. at 760.

40. Ibid. at 765.

41. Ibid. at 766.

42. Ibid. at 768.

43. Ibid. at 780 (Stevens, J., dissenting).

44. Ibid. at 784 (Stevens, J., dissenting).

45. Ibid. at 779 (Stevens, J., dissenting).

46. Lenahan (Gonzales), et al., v. United States, Case 12.626, Inter-Am. C.H.R., Report No. 80/11 (2011).

47. Ibid. at paras 109, 119, 120.

48. United Nations Human Rights Council, "Report of the Special Rapporteur on Violence Against Women, Its Causes and Consequences," June 1, 2011, www2.ohchr.org/english/bodies/hrcouncil/docs/17session/A.HRC.17.26.Add.5_AEV.pdf.

49. *Civil Rights Cases*, 109 U.S. at 27.

50. Strebeigh, *Equal*, 426.

## DISCRIMINATORY LAWS

1. Ruth Bader Ginsburg, remarks as honored guest of the "Great Lives in the Law" series at Duke University Law School, January 31, 2005.

2. Muller v. Oregon, 208 U.S. 412, 421 (1908).

3. Craig v. Boren, 429 U.S. 190 (1976).

4. Immigration and Nationality Act, 8 U.S.C. §1409(a) (2006).

5. Tuan Anh Nguyen v. INS, 533 U.S. 53, 62 (2001).

6. Ibid. at 65.

7. Ibid. at 70.

8. Ibid. at 66.

9. Ibid.

10. Ibid.

11. Ibid. at 55.

12. Ibid. at 86 (O'Connor, J., dissenting).

13. Ibid. at 92 (O'Connor, J., dissenting).

14. Ibid. at 94 (O'Connor, J., dissenting).

15. David Lamb, "Children of the Vietnam War," *Smithsonian Magazine,* June 2009.

16. Reed v. Reed, 404 U.S. 71 (1971).

17. Frontiero v. Richardson, 411 U.S. 677, 688 (1973).

18. Ibid. at 692 (Powell, J., concurring).

19. *Craig,* 429 U.S. at 200.

20. Ibid. at 223.

21. Ibid. at 201.

22. Ibid. at 214.

23. Ibid. at 204.

24. Ibid. at 210.

25. Ibid. at 211 (Powell, J., concurring).

26. Ibid. at 212 (Stevens, J., concurring).

27. Ibid. at 214 (Stevens, J., concurring).

28. Ibid. at 217 (Burger, J., dissenting).

29. Ibid. at 220 (Rehnquist, J., dissenting).

30. Ibid. at 221 (Rehnquist, J., dissenting).

31. Ibid. at 218 (Rehnquist, J., dissenting).

32. Ibid. at 219 (Rehnquist, J., dissenting).

33. Ibid. at 226 (Rehnquist, J., dissenting).

34. United States v. Virginia, 44 F.3d 1229 (Fourth Cir. 1995).

35. United States v. Virginia et al., 518 U.S. 515 (1996).

36. Faulkner v. Jones, 51 F.3d 440 (Fourth Cir. 1995).

37. Jennifer Berry Hawes, "Where Is Shannon Faulkner Now? First Female Cadet at The Citadel Talks with Oprah Again," *Post and Courier,* October 20, 2012, www.post andcourier.com/article/20121020/PC12/121029996.

38. Grove City Coll. v. Bell, 465 U.S. 555 (1984).

39. Athletics Under Title IX, www.titleix.info/10-key-areas-of-title-ix/athletics.aspx.

40. "Title IX: Facts at a Glance," ACLU, February 24, 2012, www.aclu.org/womens -rights/title-ix-facts-glance.

41. See Alexander v. Yale University, 631 F.2d 178 (Second Cir. 1980), which first found sexual harassment of female students to constitute sex discrimination and to fall within the scope of Title IX. In cases of sexual harassment, however, liability has been severely limited by the Supreme Court. See Gebser v. Lago Vista Independent School District, 524 U.S. 274, 292 (1998), where the court held in the case of a high school teacher who had a year-long sexual relationship with an eighth grader that the school could not be held liable "absent actual notice and deliberate indifference."

42. Lochner v. New York, 198 U.S. 45 (1905).

43. *Muller,* 208 U.S. at 420.

44. Ibid. at 421.

45. "State May Limit Woman's Work," *The Oregonian*, February 25, 1908 (summary available at the Oregon History Project, www.ohs.org/education/oregonhistory/historical_records/dspDocument.cfm?doc_ID=08D53543-C36D-178B-AA6FAB67DB35C200).

46. *Muller*, 208 U.S. at 421.

47. Kahn v. Shevin, 416 U.S. 351 (1974).

48. Weinberger v. Wiesenfeld, 420 U.S. 636 (1975).

49. Califano v. Webster, 430 U.S. 313, 317 (1977).

50. Califano v. Goldfarb, 430 U.S. 199 (1977).

## THE NEW ERA

1. See Abby Ferla, "ERA: Historical Curiosity or Needed Weapon Against Bias?" Remapping Debate, www.remappingdebate.org/article/era-historical-curiosity-or-needed-weapon-against-bias-today?page=0,3.

2. Ibid.

3. Idaho v. Freeman, 529 F. Supp. 1107, 1152 (D.C. Idaho 1981).

4. Ibid. at 1126.

5. Dillon v. Gloss, 256 U.S. 368, 374 (1921).

6. Ibid. at 375.

7. Ibid. at 374.

8. *Idaho*, 529 F. Supp. at 1133.

9. Ibid. at 1152.

10. Ibid. at 1153.

11. Ibid. at 1153.

12. Nebraska in 1973, Tennessee in 1974, Idaho in 1977, Kentucky in 1978, and South Dakota in 1979.

13. *Idaho*, 529 F. Supp. at 1147–48.

14. Ibid. at 1149.

15. Ibid. at 1154.

16. National Organization for Women, Inc. v. Idaho, 459 U.S. 809 (1982).

17. Despite a motion filed by the Carter administration's Department of Justice to disqualify him, Chief Judge Marion Callister refused to recuse himself from the case because of a possible conflict of interest caused by his status as a highly placed officer in the Church of Jesus Christ of Latter-Day Saints (the Mormon Church), which had publicly and actively opposed the Equal Rights Amendment. Idaho v. Freeman, 478 F. Supp. 33 (D. Idaho 1979).

18. Allison L. Held, Sheryl L. Herndon, and Danielle M. Stager, "The Equal Rights Amendment: Why the ERA Remains Legally Viable and Properly Before the States." *William and Mary Journal of Women and the Law* 3, no. 1 (Spring 1997).

19. See VoteERA.org.

20. Alaska, California, Colorado, Connecticut, Florida, Hawaii, Illinois, Iowa, Louisiana, Maryland, Massachusetts, Montana, New Hampshire, New Jersey, New Mexico, Pennsylvania, Rhode Island, Texas, Utah, Virginia, Washington, and Wyoming.

21. See Linda J. Wharton, "State Equal Rights Amendments Revisited: Evaluating Their Effectiveness in Advancing Protection against Sex Discrimination," *Rutgers Law Journal* 36, no. 4 (2005).

22. Ibid., 1248–49.

# PUBLISHING IN THE PUBLIC INTEREST

Thank you for reading this book published by The New Press. The New Press is a nonprofit, public interest publisher. New Press books and authors play a crucial role in sparking conversations about the key political and social issues of our day.

We hope you enjoyed this book and that you will stay in touch with The New Press. Here are a few ways to stay up to date with our books, events, and the issues we cover:

- Sign up at www.thenewpress.com/subscribe to receive updates on New Press authors and issues and to be notified about local events
- Like us on Facebook: www.facebook.com/newpressbooks
- Follow us on Twitter: www.twitter.com/thenewpress

Please consider buying New Press books for yourself; for friends and family; or to donate to schools, libraries, community centers, prison libraries, and other organizations involved with the issues our authors write about.

The New Press is a 501(c)(3) nonprofit organization. You can also support our work with a tax-deductible gift by visiting www.thenew press.com/donate.